Y0-BGG-931

FUSION

I'm with you 2:
Raising a bilingual child in a two-language household

Written and published by

Glen Taylor

LIBRARY AND ARCHIVES CANADA CATALOGUING IN PUBLICATION

Taylor, Glen
    Fusion : I'm with you 2: Raising a bilingual child in a two-language household / Glen Taylor.

Includes bibliographical references and index.
ISBN 978-0-9784276-0-3

    1. Canadians, French-speaking—Education.
2. Bilingualism—Canada. 3. Biculturalism. 4. French language—Acquisition. 5. Language acquisition—Parent participation. I. Title.

LC3734.T392 2007   371.829'114071   C2007-904745-9

Illustrations: François Richardier
                  www3.telus.net/artstudio42
Printing: K.J. Millar Production
Distribution: Exogamie au Canada / Exogamy in Canada
                  www.exogam.ca

All rights reserved. No part of this book may be reproduced in any form or by any electronic or mechanical means, including information storage and retrieval systems, without permission in writing from the publisher.

Copyright © 2007 Glen Taylor
Illustrations copyright © 2007 François Richardier

Je dédie ce livre à ma conjointe Christine, avec qui je mène une très belle vie de couple exogame, ainsi qu'à mes deux filles bilingues, Éléonore et Isabelle, qui démontrent si bien la richesse de fusionner deux langues et deux cultures.

I dedicate this book to my spouse, Christine, with whom I share a wonderful life as an exogamous couple, and to my two bilingual daughters, Eleonore and Isabelle, who so beautifully embody the fusion of two languages and cultures.

About the author

Glen Taylor is the non-francophone half of an exogamous couple and the father of two children who attend a French-language school in Calgary. He is the author of the original version of *I'm with you!* and the editor of *ConnEXions*, the first and only magazine for mixed couples in Canada.

Since the 2002 publication of *I'm with you!*, Glen has dedicated himself to helping build understanding among parents and educators in French-language school systems across Canada. Among his numerous projects, he has trained "EX Teams"— resource people who work with exogamous couples—in British Columbia and Ontario, written a variety of resource material, and given a host of presentations and workshops throughout the country to parents, teachers and administrators.

Glen holds a BA in French from Université Laval (Quebec City) and an MA in Translation from the Université de Montréal.

His website, Exogamie au Canada / Exogamy in Canada, can be found at **www.exogam.ca**.

Acknowledgements

I wish to thank all the people I have met over the years in my exogamy-related projects; your ideas, insights and commitment are a constant source of inspiration. In particular, thanks go to the following people who have provided encouragement, expertise and feedback:

Marie-Andrée Asselin
Josée Bergeron
Randy Boras
Michelle Boucher
Francine Ciccarelli
Lynda Clark
Ricky Coté
Michelle Daveluy
Lyse Deselliers
Heather Desrosiers
Jacqueline Dorval
Brigitte Duguay Langlais
Geneviève Folliet
Carole Forbes
Jean-Paul Gagner
Marc Gignac
Ken Hill
Rachelle Hill
Marie-Carmel Jean-Jacques
Corinne Jolicoeur

Todd Jolicoeur
Lorne Kelton
Lucie Lavoie
Jocelyne L'Ecuyer
Brigitte Lefebvre-Malyon
Treena Lepage
Michelle Marsan
Al Matchett
Mike McKean
Julie Moran
John O'Shaughnessy
Hélène Pouliot-Cleare
Mimi Richard-Golding
Suzanne Rochon
Ginette Roy
Lise Roy
Charlaine Savard
Laurie Stone
Denise Summerfield
Garth Williams

I wish to thank my daughters Isabelle and Eleonore for helping to find the name *Fusion*, and Eleonore for her invaluable assistance in preparing the manuscript.

I'd like to express special thanks to Andrée Bélanger-Major, Anne-Marie Boucher, Phyllis Dalley, Henri Lemire and Claire Thibideau. Our many discussions about exogamy and French-language education have helped broaden my understanding immensely.

Lastly, thank you to the board of the Fédération des parents francophones de l'Alberta for agreeing that I should take the book *I'm with you!* into its next incarnation.

Foreword

When I wrote the original version[1] of *I'm with you!* for the Fédération des parents francophones de l'Alberta in 2002, French-language school boards and parent associations were just starting to deal with the issues raised by exogamous, or mixed, couples. Actually, some were starting; others hadn't even reached that point yet.

Five years have passed, during which I have had the pleasure of giving a wide variety of presentations and meeting scores of parents in every region of Canada. I have also collaborated with educators, administrators and researchers in an effort to help non-French-speaking parents play a more active role in their children's education. All of this exogamy-related work has helped broaden my understanding of the issues and develop a level of nuance that I now find is missing from *I'm with you!*.

The present book started out as a simple revision of *I'm with you!*—one that percolated in my mind for over a year before I finally set pen to paper. Once begun, however, the task took on a whole new dimension: although certain elements of the original book were still relevant, I wanted to add others that reflected the questions and concerns I had heard from parents and educators.

In the following pages, you'll find a host of information about raising your child to be one of those amazing individuals who can switch between two languages with the greatest of ease, and whose outlook on life is profoundly influenced by their ability to interpret the world around them using two sets of cultural references.

I hope readers will find this new book both informative and entertaining. If you have questions or comments, feel free to visit the *Exogamie au Canada / Exogamy in Canada* website at **www.exogam.ca**.

---

[1] The original version of *I'm with you!* was published in 2002 by the Fédération des parents francophones de l'Alberta; an abridged version was subsequently released by the Fédération nationale des conseils scolaires francophones and the Centre ontarien de ressources pédagogiques.

Table of contents

Welcome to FUSION

One day, when I had almost finished writing this book, I asked my two daughters to help me find a title. I wanted something that reflected their reality as well as that of our family: a francophone parent (my spouse), an anglophone parent (me), and children who are both francophone and anglophone—yet who, when pressed, call themselves something else: "bilingual."

My children aren't the only offspring of mixed couples to use this label. Over the past few years, I've met many young people who have fully developed the incredible potential that comes from having parents with different mother tongues.

Children who develop this potential speak, read and write French as well as any other francophone and English as well as any other anglophone. In other words, they have two mother tongues—something that is increasingly common in Canada's francophone communities. Depending on their parents' origins, some children grow up with other mother tongues as well.

Since language is intricately linked to culture, these children develop an identity that combines each of their parents' cultural backgrounds. They see the world around them through the eyes of someone who perceives, interprets, and expresses him- or herself instinctively in French, and through the eyes of someone who perceives, interprets, and expresses him- or herself instinctively in English. Some children have a different or an additional set of cultural references as well.

The fusion of their linguistic and cultural heritage results in an identity that isn't easy to label, and is even harder to define mathematically. Why? Because these children develop a sort of "hybrid" identity, the whole of which is far greater than the sum of its parts. They aren't 50 percent francophone and 50 percent anglophone: rather, they're 100 percent of both. That's what they mean when they say, "I'm bilingual."

Impressive, isn't it? As we'll see in the following pages, though, children are perfectly able to accomplish this amazing feat with very little difficulty. In fact, the challenge is more for us than for them...

What you'll find in this book

Have you heard or used the word *exogamy* lately? It's a term that seems to pop up whenever people involved in French-language education get together. Once you've finished reading Chapter 1, you'll know more about the word *exogamy* than...

a) anyone else in your home
b) anyone on your block
c) everyone you know
d) millions of Canadians
e) billions of people around the world
f) you actually wanted to know.

That's just the beginning (*phew!*); after that, we'll take a look at how exogamy applies to your family life. Then there's a chapter about children's development—some pretty amazing stuff happens when our kids are young!

If you survive up to that point, you'll find a more down-to-earth chapter about what you can do at home to help your child develop her or his awesome potential. That's Chapter 4; you'll find more ideas for helping your child inside and outside school in Chapter 6. Sandwiched between the two is a chapter that looks into the various educational options you have for your child, particularly that of French-language schooling.

Finally, in Chapter 7, we'll visit a part of the world that your child will inhabit if you and your spouse so desire: the Francophonie. More specifically, you'll be able to learn a bit about francophone life in each province and territory of Canada.

Of course, you can always jump to whatever section seems most appropriate at any given time. If you're looking for specific information on a given topic, the index at the back of the book might help.

About the subtitle...

When I chose *Raising a bilingual child in a two-language household* as the subtitle for this book, I was thinking of the children I've described above. I've been telling mixed couples in workshops and presentations for five years now that their youngsters have the potential to develop two mother tongues, one of which is French. The biggest challenge those parents face in that respect is helping their children master French and develop a solid francophone component to their identity. That doesn't mean English or another language isn't equally important! It's just the reality of francophones who live in a mostly English-speaking environment.

Mixed couples who create a two-language household provide their children with the foundation they need to become fully, fluently, wonderfully bilingual. Unfortunately for many youngsters, this seems to be easier said than done. I hope that some of the information and ideas in the following pages will strike a chord with parents who aren't yet sure what they want for their children and how to go about making it happen.

I've written this book in English in order to reach as many mixed couples as possible.

Un mot aux parents francophones

J'espère vivement que les parents francophones de couple mixte trouveront dans les pages suivantes des informations et des idées valables malgré le fait qu'elles soient présentées en anglais. Mon but n'est nullement de compromettre la nature française du foyer mixte ni des écoles de langue française mais plutôt de sensibiliser les parents non francophones et de les inciter à participer pleinement à l'épanouissement équilibré de leur enfant. Comme vous allez voir, un élément clé de cette participation est l'appui actif de l'apprentissage du français et de la construction identitaire francophone des enfants.

Êtes-vous Acadienne ou Acadien?

Les Acadiennes et Acadiens se distinguent au sein de la francophonie canadienne pour des raisons historiques, linguistiques et culturelles. Tout en reconnaissant cette spécificité identitaire, il y a certains passages dans le présent livre où nous incluons implicitement la collectivité acadienne dans l'étiquette *francophone* uniquement afin d'alléger le texte.

A word to single parents

Were you once part of a mixed couple and are now raising your child either alone or jointly with your ex? If so, the "two-language household" in the subtitle still applies to you. For instance, if you have joint custody, your child's "household" simply includes two addresses. Sure, it makes things more complicated, but the fact remains that your youngster has the potential to become bilingual.

One last word

FUSION is all about the richness that comes from having two mother tongues. It's also about helping our children realize this extraordinary potential from which they'll benefit all their lives.

Enjoy!

1. Exogamy

You might be surprised to learn that *exogamy* isn't on everyone's Favourite Words list. Hard to believe, we know. But we'll be using it throughout this book because it's just so... handy! First, though, let's start with a few words about *that word*.

What's in a word?

Exogamy is used in anthropological circles to mean "marriage outside one's own community, clan, or tribe."[1] It applies to the practice of prohibiting marriage between two members of the same group (clan, tribe, etc.) in order to prevent inbreeding and to foster greater harmony between groups. The definition implies that each individual in a given group, whether by birth or by marriage, is a member of that group only.

Now, let's muddy the waters:

> In the context of Canada's official-language duality, *exogamy* can mean "union of two individuals with different mother tongues and cultural backgrounds."

More often than not, the term is used to describe the union of a francophone and an anglophone, reflecting the country's two official languages.

Like many things in life, the definition isn't perfect. For instance, it suggests that language and culture can be wrapped up and put into neat little boxes—as in, "All anglophones speak the same language and have the same culture." Try telling that to a farmer on the rolling plains of Saskatchewan and a fisher on the rolling seas of Newfoundland and Labrador. What if someone has more than one mother tongue, and what exactly is a "cultural background" anyway?

---

[1] *Canadian Oxford Dictionary*, Second Edition. (Oxford University Press, 2004).

Despite the imperfections, let's forge ahead with an even more specific definition:

> **For the purposes of this book, *exogamy* will mean "union of a francophone and a non-francophone to form a married or common-law couple."**

Ah yes, the worms are already wriggling out of the can. What makes someone a francophone? We'd need to clarify that minor detail before going on to define a non-francophone, wouldn't we. Is it a matter of language, culture, family heritage, or a combination thereof? If it's cultural, how does one define culture? If it's family heritage, how far back in the family tree should one look?

They're valid questions, but we won't even try to answer them at this point. Let's just say there are two main reasons for this definition:

1. **This book is intended for couples made up of...**
   a) someone who, when it comes to his or her children's educational options, is considered a francophone (see Chapter 5 for more information on schooling options and the right to a francophone education), and
   b) a partner who, in that context, doesn't wear the "francophone" label.

2. **That partner may identify him- or herself as belonging to...**
   a) the English-speaking majority, and/or
   b) any other non-French-speaking linguistic or cultural group.

The definition applies to common-law and married couples, but it says nothing about whether those couples are living together.

> If you were once part of a mixed couple, you can still enrich your child's life by exposing her or him to both languages and cultures, to the best of your abilities and in light of your particular circumstances. The challenges you face will probably be greater, but you'll find teachers and other parents who will be there to help you. We hope this book proves useful as well, since it's intended for you, too!

How do you pronounce that word?

Exogamy is pronounced "eggs-<u>aw</u>-ga-mee." The adjective is *exogamous*, and it's pronounced "eggs-<u>aw</u>-ga-mous." In French, the noun is *exogamie*, and the adjective is *exogame* (singular) or *exogames* (plural). For some reason we have yet to fathom, the word seems to pose fewer pronunciation problems *en français* than it does in English.

Perhaps it's the pronunciation that turns some people off this lovely word. Judging from different reactions we've seen, the English version seems to conjure up images of a nasty variety of the flu, whereas in French, it sounds more like an exotic skin infection. We'd be tempted to suggest the French language seems a bit more—how can we put this diplomatically?—*refined* than English, but in this case, we'd have to admit that neither alternative is particularly appealing.

It's possible that some of your family, friends or acquaintances consider the accent on the "aw" in *exogamy* to be a bad sign, as in, "Aw, couldn't you find someone who speaks *our* language?" (implied message: "That's <u>aw</u>ful!"). People who react this way also tend to insist that only one language—theirs—be spoken in their presence (especially in their home), and who bristle like offended porcupines whenever another language is used within their otherwise peaceful little bubble.

If you run into folks who dislike the mixing of languages and cultures, don't let it get to you. Just remember that the accent on the "aw" in *exogamy* actually refers to something much more positive: "<u>Aw</u>esome!"

"But what if I don't like that word?"

So you're one of the few (okay, the few thousand) people who don't like *exogamous*, and you're looking for an alternative. *Mixed* is a term some people prefer, though it's not particularly specific; it could imply the blending of two single-parent families, or the union of two individuals with different racial backgrounds but the same language, or two people with different religions, and so on. Variations on the theme include "linguistically mixed," "culturally mixed" and "totally mixed up," but we won't be using them here.

> For the sake of variety, we will use *mixed* as a synonym for *exogamous* in this book. As for the "mixed" equivalent of *exogamy*, well, there really isn't one, so we're still stuck with the latter.

What about *interlinguistic* and *intercultural*? Somewhat awkward, aren't they? Plus they're both covered succinctly by the single term *exogamous* as we've defined it, so we won't use them either.

Finally, for those of you who dislike all of the above, feel free to use the variants *mixtogamy* and *mixtogamous* (*mixtogamie* and *mixtogame(s)* in French), though they aren't actually recognized words yet—they're just fun to say.

Using that word

Exogamy and *exogamous* are often misused, or are used so loosely that their meaning becomes somewhat obscured. For the record, here are a few simple guidelines on how you can use *exogamy* and *exogamous* accurately to impress and amaze family, friends, acquaintances and total strangers:

⇒ Couples can be exogamous.

⇒ Individuals cannot be exogamous.

⇒ Families cannot be exogamous either; this sort of union applies only to couples.

⇒ *Exogamous household* can be used to describe the home situation of mixed couples and their offspring.

⇒ *Exogamous marriage*, while correct, isn't something you'd want to put on the wedding or anniversary invitations.

Why such a fuss over a simple word?

We're making all this fuss in order to make a couple of points. First of all, *exogamy* is often used—and misused—as a simple word, whereas in fact it describes a highly complex reality. Considering that the very notion of *francophone* is increasingly open to interpretation, a word like *exogamy*, with its imperfect definition, should be used with care.

The decision to form a mixed couple, and then a family, can be more complicated than one might think. In the past, it was often greeted with dismay, disappointment and even hostility from people on all sides. It can still elicit similar reactions today, though they seem to occur much less frequently. Gone are the days when people wouldn't dare venture outside their own village, community, clan or tribe!

> While exogamy makes life interesting in a hundred ways for couples as well as their immediate and extended families, the growing number of mixed households is also having a significant impact on French-language schools and francophone communities across the country.

These are just some of the reasons for spending so much time discussing the word *exogamy*. Even more important is this: **for the purposes of French-language education, every child born to a francophone parent as defined in the Charter of Rights and Freedoms is a francophone.** (You can learn more about the Charter of Rights and Freedoms in Chapter 5.)

It doesn't matter if that parent has formed a couple with another francophone or with a partner who has a different language and culture. That's why families can't be called exogamous: the couple is exogamous, the children are francophones...

... which is, of course, just the beginning of the discussion—or rather, the beginning of many discussions. For instance, if francophone parents choose not to pass on their language and culture to their children, do those children cease to be francophones at some point?

As for the children of mixed couples, does their identity not also include the language and culture associated with their other parent? Do labels such as "francophone," "anglophone" and "allophone" adequately describe those children, or are there other terms that fit better? How about mixed couples themselves: for the purposes of francophone education, aren't both partners also francophones?

We hope the following pages will give you and your partner some food for thought. It's a fascinating world you've entered, and well worth taking time to explore.

In a nutshell...

For the purposes of this book, *exogamy* means "union of a francophone and a non-francophone who form a married or common-law couple." Underlying the term is a complex reality that touches not only couples and their families, but also the francophone communities in which they live.

2. Family ties

If you and your spouse form a mixed couple and you're either planning or are already raising children, how would you describe your family? Is it like the one you grew up in? Or like that of your spouse? If not, are the differences minor or major? For instance, if you grew up in a single-language household and are now raising kids in a two-language home, we'd call that a major difference.

People generally don't dwell on questions like this, especially when their children are younger. After all, who has the time? Adding a new member to a family requires a real adjustment, and the dynamics are constantly shifting and evolving. Any such description, then, is more like a snapshot in time—but it is definitely a valuable exercise nonetheless.

Deciding how to raise children is sometimes a source of concern, and even friction, between exogamous couples and members of their respective families. For instance, how many grandparents worry that their grandchildren won't be able to speak their language? It helps to have reflected and become informed before you start discussing such matters with family and friends.

So, if you were filling out a form and had to describe your family in 214 words (the length of these four paragraphs), what would you write?

Take time to talk

The first place to start discussing these questions, of course, is at home with your spouse. Raising children in two languages and cultures requires understanding, respect and solidarity between the parents. In addition to the usual issues all couples face, there are a host of other questions that, sooner or later, must be answered.

You'll find a few such questions on the next page. You and your spouse might want to use them as a starting point in your discussions.

Question	Yes	No
Would you want your child to grow up speaking your mother tongue?		
Why or why not?		
Would you want your child to grow up speaking your spouse's mother tongue?		
Why or why not?		
Would you want your child to grow up speaking both mother tongues fluently?		
Why or why not?		
Would it bother you if your child wasn't able to speak your mother tongue?		
Why or why not?		
Would it bother you if your child wasn't able to speak your spouse's mother tongue?		
Why or why not?		
Do you and your spouse see any differences between your respective cultures?		
What are some examples?		
Are there any elements of your culture you would absolutely want to pass on to your child?		
Which ones, and why?		
Are there any elements of your spouse's culture you would absolutely want to pass on to your child?		
Which ones, and why?		
Are there any elements of your culture you really would not want to pass on to your child?		
Which ones, and why?		
Are there any elements of your spouse's culture you really would not want to pass on to your child?		
Which ones, and why?		
Would you want your child to grow up with both cultures?		
If so, why? If not, why not?		

These are just a few of the questions that arise when children enter into a mixed couple's life. They may be short (the questions, that is), but answering them means delving deep into each person's beliefs and values—and the answers are sometimes surprising.

When you and your spouse discuss these matters, you'll find that questions about language and culture lead to other questions about education, including:

Question	Yes	No
Would you want your child to be educated in English?		
Why or why not?		
Would you want your child to be educated in French?		
Why or why not?		
If you and your spouse want your child to be educated in French, would you choose a francophone school or an immersion program?		
Why?		
If you and your spouse opted for francophone education, would you want your child to change into an English school after kindergarten?		
Why or why not?		
After Grade 3?		
Why or why not?		
After grades 6, 7, 8 or 9?		
Why or why not?		
If either you or your spouse has a different mother tongue and there's a possibility to have your child educated in that language, would you choose that option?		
Why or why not?		

Once again, your answers will reveal what you believe and value. It's not always easy to discuss questions like these, but couples who don't do so when their children are young may well regret their silence later on.

More about language

You and your spouse likely struck up a relationship using a single language with which you both felt comfortable. Statistics show that English is the most common language used by mixed couples outside Quebec.[2] One language is enough for many couples until they decide to have children.

> There's a saying among francophones living in a predominantly English setting: "Children need to be taught French; as for English, they just catch it!"

Hmm… like a cold, perhaps? Or like Harry Potter's elusive Golden Snitch? Whatever the reference may be, the fact is that couples made up of two francophones who speak only French at home and send their children to a French-language school are  often astounded at how quickly their children pick up English.

WELL, WELL, ANDRÉ, IT LOOKS LIKE YOU FINALLY CAUGHT ENGLISH!

Mixed couples who decide they want their children to grow up with two mother tongues and two cultures face a certain number of challenges. For example, when English is spoken virtually everywhere outside their home, and especially when it's the language used between the parents, how can they ensure equal opportunity for French?

---

[2] *Mother Tongue vs. Home Language.* (Statistics Canada, 2001 Census).

OPOL

One answer is OPOL: One Parent, One Language. This approach to bilingual childrearing has been around for a long time; it involves each parent speaking his or her mother tongue consistently with the children.

This may sound easy, but sometimes francophones who have always spoken English with their spouse will feel too awkward to start speaking French at home. With their spouse's understanding and support, however, these parents can overcome their self-consciousness and establish a long-term language habit with their child.

> If your spouse is a francophone, encourage her or him to speak French with your children all the time. The OPOL goal is to create a habit rather than a rigid rule; it should feel *natural* for children to communicate with their francophone parent in French.

The francophone parent who consistently speaks French with his or her child helps that youngster develop a solid language base. The non-francophone parent who actively encourages and supports this language habit also helps the child develop French-language abilities that will last a lifetime.

This is just one example of how non-French-speaking parents can contribute to their children's French-language learning. In so doing, they help their children become fully bilingual. What could be more fitting for children with two sets of roots?

Considering that it can sometimes be a challenge for two francophone parents to maintain a balance between French and English in their home, especially with teens, just imagine what it's like when only one parent speaks French!

If your mother tongue is English, you have a built-in language support network: the English-speaking society around you. If your mother tongue is neither French nor English, you can pass your language on to your children by always speaking to them in that language.

In a nutshell...

The biggest challenge facing mixed couples in a predominantly English-speaking setting is to ensure that their children master French. That's why it's so important for the francophone parent to speak the language consistently with the children, and for the non-francophone parent to encourage this language habit.

Culture and exogamy

Language is a vehicle by which culture evolves and gets passed on through the generations. But what exactly is culture? There's no simple answer.

> The *Canadian Encyclopedia* compiled over 160 definitions before creating its own: "an ensemble, formalized in varying degrees, of ways of thinking, feeling and behaving which once learned give people a particular and distinct collectivity."[3]

Visit a minority francophone school anywhere in Canada, and you'll see a "particular collectivity"!

The role culture plays in mixed households depends on each parent's background and priorities. How many francophones have introduced their spouses to French cuisine, and how many anglophones have happily added this ingredient to their daily lives? How many French-English families enjoy a *réveillon* on Christmas Eve, and then celebrate Christmas the next day, too?

How many youngsters of exogamous couples know the nursery rhymes of each parent's language? And what about the countless customs and traditions associated with other linguistic and cultural communities?

Culture is part of our identity, and it's with us from our early years. The songs we sing to our children when they're small are often the same ones our parents sang to us. Although we can't easily define culture, culture is something that defines each and every one of us.

---

[3] *The Canadian Encylopedia*. (Historica, 2007).

Culture is far more complex and varied than we might think, too. Just as anglophone culture varies considerably across Canada, so does francophone culture: Franco-Albertans are different from Franco-Ontarians or *Ontarois*, who are different from Fransaskois, and so on.

> Many francophone communities are also enriched by the presence of families with different ethnic backgrounds. Add all these elements together, and you've got a world of variety within what's called "francophone culture."

Acadians distinguish themselves among French-speaking Canadians for historical, linguistic and cultural reasons. Ontario's francophone population tends to be divided into three regions—North, East and South—and each has characteristics that set it apart from the others. In Alberta, many francophones in the central, northeast and northwest regions can trace their Albertan roots back several generations, whereas the francophones in the south of the province tend to be more recent arrivals. As a result, the culture in each region is different.

> The francophone population of every province and territory has cultural particularities. Even individual communities within the same region can have their own cultural identities, which may be reflected in their schools.

There's also something that sets francophones living in a minority context apart from francophones who are in a majority situation, whether they're from Quebec or a French-speaking country. Services and opportunities that majority-population residents take for granted are often available to francophones in a minority setting only because those people made them happen.

Despite the myriad regional differences, francophones across Canada do share elements of a collective culture, and have some institutional tools, such as education, to help meet their needs.

They also share a language that, although it has official status federally (and provincially in New Brunswick), seems to be losing ground on Canada's linguistic landscape. Many francophones outside Quebec are acutely aware that their language needs to be vigorously defended and promoted. Some will even turn to the courts if they have to.

That's a lot of baggage!

Francophones outside Quebec live with a constant threat of assimilation. There are also plenty of misperceptions among anglophones across Canada as well as francophones in Quebec. A case in point: a Quebec premier once referred to francophones outside his province as "dead ducks"—hardly an encouraging (or informed) assessment.

> One of the characteristics of francophones living in a minority setting is that they're incredibly dynamic!

Maintaining a vibrant francophone language and culture in a minority setting is an ongoing struggle that most majority-language speakers, whether English or French, know little about. If you get involved in your child's francophone education, you'll be able to gain firsthand knowledge of this struggle.

Remember, your children will inherit all this francophone "cultural baggage" as well as the culture you pass on to them. Theirs will be a highly complex blend of dreams, hopes and challenges that evolves over time. In fact, it's likely that their culture will be a unique blend of elements

from your background and from that of your spouse.

If you and your spouse fundamentally appreciate each other's language and culture, you'll be better able to understand and guide your children as they grow up.

Language, culture and education

Couples comprising at least one francophone parent have the right to send their children to a French-language school. Research shows that children with francophone roots—whether or not both parents are French-speaking—can develop highly balanced bilingualism if French language and culture are promoted at home and at their school.[4] The emphasis not only on language but also on culture is one of the most compelling reasons for enrolling your child in a French-language school.

---

4 Rodrigue Landry and Réal Allard, "L'exogamie et le maintien de deux langues et de deux cultures : le rôle de la francité familioscolaire." (*Revue des sciences de l'éducation*, Vol. 23, No. 3, 1997), p. 587.

In a nutshell...

Children of mixed couples have the potential to become fluently bilingual and identify with francophone and anglophone (or another) culture. They can do this when both parents respect and actively support each other's language and cultural heritage. Studies show that parents also help when they encourage the use of French at home and enrol their children in a French-language school.

"What's best for our child?"

It's not always easy to be objective, especially when it comes to making important decisions for our children. We're influenced by our own reality, which means our own successes, failures, hopes, fears, aspirations, apprehensions, and so on. This is only natural, but at the same time all those influences can make it difficult to answer a deceivingly simple question: "What's best for our child?"

> Exogamous couples face unique challenges—and opportunities—brought about by the presence of two languages and cultures in their home.

The questions we saw in the previous section are part of a larger discussion:

Do we want our child to be anglophone, francophone, bilingual, bicultural... or do we want her or him to combine both our languages and cultures?

What does it mean to be francophone or anglophone; are they mutually exclusive, or rather components of a single identity?

What's the best way for youngsters to develop their language skills?

What does each of us want to pass on to our child more than anything else?

How does all this fit into his or her overall development?

Labels are suitable for jars...

We're using labels here like they're the only way to describe people—which they're not! They are, however, a handy tool for representing different realities. For our purposes, let's consider an anglophone as someone who identifies with the collectivity of individuals whose mother tongue and primary culture is English. A francophone, on the other hand, identifies with the collectivity whose mother tongue and primary culture is French.

... but not for people!

Yes, we know these definitions leave much to be desired. We've met children of mixed couples who are neither only anglophone nor only francophone, but a seamless blend—a fusion—of both. Not only do they master both languages, but their perception of the world reflects the influence of two sets of cultural references.

> The notion of a hybrid identity raises questions and even concern among some educators, not to mention debate among researchers. As parents in mixed couples, however, it can be immensely satisfying to know that our children have fully integrated both sets of family roots.

In order to bring "hybridism" into our discussion, we occasionally refer to "components" when speaking of francophone, anglophone or other linguistic and cultural references. And since people's identities are influenced so profoundly by language and culture, we've dedicated the next chapter to exploring children's development.

Ultimately, the approach that works for your couple will depend on what each of you thinks is best for your child. Some parents want their youngsters to become bilingual anglophones, while others hope to raise bilingual francophones. Certain couples want their children to become so fluently bilingual and bicultural that they'll see themselves as both—the so-called "hybrids" we mentioned earlier. Then there are those who'd rather see their children have a single language and culture—inevitably that of the English-speaking majority.

Parents' attitudes can vary enormously. But they usually aren't set in stone; they evolve as people reflect and learn more. They can also change when parents focus—really focus—on what's best for their children.

> It's something we have to ask ourselves over and over—and over—again when making decisions on our children's future. This may seem obvious, but it really isn't. It takes a constant effort to look beyond our own influences in order to see things from our children's point of view in the short, medium and long term.

What's important to keep in mind is that your children have a unique potential to develop a blend of two languages and cultures from the moment they're born. How you help them develop this potential is up to you.

But remember: it's *their* potential, and *your* responsibility to do what's best for them!

In a nutshell...

Although it seems obvious, it isn't always easy to keep focused on this simple question: "What's best for our child?" Making the most appropriate decisions for children means constantly thinking of what would be best for them in the short, medium and long term.

3. Growing up

An a-maze-ing story

Imagine a vast maze made up of virtually limitless channels that wind around, double back, crisscross, and come together at every conceivable angle and from every possible direction. Now add a steady stream of vehicles of every size and shape, driven by single-minded (if not crazily obsessed) individuals, each with one goal: to get from Point A to Point B as quickly as possible.

As you might expect, all this frenzied activity has a major impact on the maze: certain routes get widened into freeways to accommodate heavier traffic flow, timesaving shortcuts are opened up between other channels, and less-travelled lanes eventually become dead ends.

Now, some of you might think we're describing Toronto's road system. Not so! Rather, this is an illustration of what's happening inside your child's brain as he or she grows. Babies are born with billions of neurons—cells that transmit information throughout the body's nervous system. For those neurons to work properly, they have to form hundreds of trillions of connections, or synapses, many of which are concentrated in the brain.

The madly dashing vehicles are actually bits of information, and they're rushing in from various sources including the senses (sight, hearing, smell, touch and taste) for processing by the brain. The heavily travelled routes and useful shortcuts are interconnected synapses created between more frequently used neurons. As for the dead ends, they're former channels where the neurons just didn't get enough use.

Like any good road network, the more freeways there are, the more efficiently information can circulate throughout the system.

Wiring and pruning

Contrary to what people used to think, children's brains don't develop in a steadily increasing, or linear, manner. In fact, the first few years of life are an astonishingly busy time for synapse creation: a two-year-old will have developed as many connections as an adult, and a year later, the number of synapses in that little head will have doubled, reaching a quadrillion! The high level of neuron activity lasts roughly for the first decade of life.

> Yes, you've read correctly: our young kids have more connections in their brains than we do. It's a bit of a sobering thought, isn't it!

So what happens between childhood and adulthood? Well, while this spectacular growth in connections—let's call it "wiring"—is going on, another process, which we'll call "pruning," is also taking place. Remember those less-travelled lanes? They get pruned into former lanes... ex-lanes... dearly departed lanes... dead ends.

The two processes wage a fierce battle for supremacy in children's brains for about a decade. In the first three years, Wiring wins decisively; then, for seven long years, the two forces are locked in a struggle of equals. After that, though, Pruning takes over and it's downhill from then on. When the dust eventually settles, the connections left standing (or working) are those that have been used so often they're now protected from the pruning process. They number a mere 500 trillion, and they're all we've got for the rest of our lives.

The silver lining to this ominous grey cloud is the fact that we end up with a more efficient network of freeways instead of an oversupply of potential pathways. But is there anything we can do to help our kids develop as many synapse superhighways as possible?

Use 'em or lose 'em

In two words, the answer is this: Use Them. As parents, you can become allies with the Forces of Connectedness by first providing your infant with a healthy, safe and caring environment. That's the best setting in which to learn. Then build on that foundation by adding positive experiences that bring into play different senses and sensations.

For example, reading to a child who is sitting in your lap brings together sights and sounds related to the book as well as the senses of touch (your combined warmth, the feel of the book) and smell (human and paper). This seemingly simple activity stimulates different parts of the brain and leads to the creation of a complex network of connections, including those needed for abstract thought. Repeating the experience will help reinforce the network to the point where the synapses no longer risk being pruned.[5]

As for mixed couples...

The amazing development that takes place in children's brains from the moment they're born (and even before) presents a fantastic opportunity for mixed couples. If parents can directly affect their infants' wiring process by simply reading to them, just imagine how beneficial it can be to expose them to two languages!

> As you might expect, a couple that exposes children to two mother tongues from birth actually helps them develop and reinforce more complex connections in their brain. Consistently using two languages will help reinforce those connections so much that they'll be protected from pruning. And recent research shows that children benefit well into their old age!

[5] Margaret Norrie McCain & J. Fraser Mustard, 1999, *Early Years Study: Reversing the Real Brain Drain.* (Study prepared for the Ontario Children's Secretariat, 1999), p. 41.

In a nutshell...

A tremendous amount of activity occurs in children's brains from the moment they're born. Parents help their youngsters build stronger and more complex neurological connections and networks when they provide a safe, healthy and caring home environment. Exogamous couples further help when each parent speaks his or her mother tongue consistently to the children. Enhanced neurological activity benefits children their entire lifetime.

Language use and identity

All kids are geniuses—just ask their parents! Seriously, though, youngsters often do amaze adults in a variety of ways, one of which is related to their use of language.

Here's where the children of mixed couples have the potential to shine: they're born into a family where they can learn two mother tongues, and maybe more. For those of us who have muddled and struggled with language in school or on trips, it's nothing short of incredible to see youngsters who are so fluently bilingual they can switch from language to another without skipping a beat.

Shaping and reflecting

The way we use language reflects who we are and how we perceive the world around us. At the same time, the language(s) present in that world also help shape who we are. A child growing up in a unilingual environment will have one set of language references; a bilingual child will have two.

How does children's language use influence their identity development? The following graphic illustrates the three spheres of language use: oral communications (listening and speaking), reading and writing. Children develop oral communications first, then learn to read and write as they grow older.

> All three skills are central to learning and to succeeding not only in school, but in life.

The first diagram illustrates the language situation of a unilingual child growing up in a unilingual environment.

Diagram 1
Unilingual child growing up in a unilingual setting

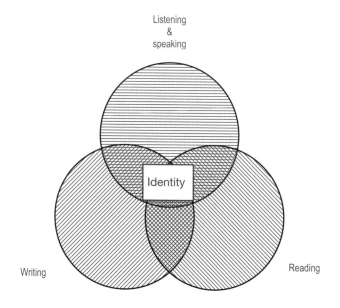

Listening & speaking

Identity

Writing

Reading

Each sphere of language use influences the other two spheres, and all three help shape the child's identity. In turn, the child expresses that identity using all three spheres of language use. (The assumption is that the child will fully develop his or her skills in each sphere.) The result is a symmetrical whole.

The children of exogamous couples have the potential to develop at least two mother tongues. The following diagram illustrates what happens when they fully develop that potential.

Diagram 2
Bilingual child growing up in a bilingual setting

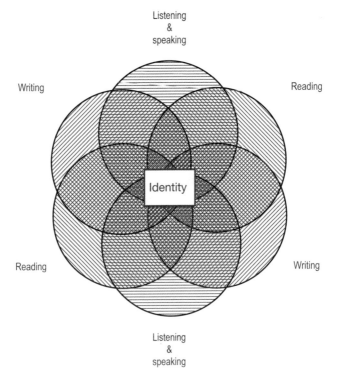

Listening & speaking

Writing

Reading

Identity

Reading

Writing

Listening & speaking

In this diagram, each sphere of language use (Listening & speaking, Reading, Writing) appears twice to reflect the presence of two languages in the child's life.

For argument's sake, let's say these two languages are French and English. Thus, one circle marked "Listening and speaking" would apply to the amount of French the child speaks and hears, while the other circle marked "Listening and speaking" would apply to the amount of English the child speaks and hears. The Reading and Writing spheres would reflect this potential duality also.

The presence of two languages in the child's environment adds several layers of complexity to his or her language situation. Once again, the spheres all overlap and help to shape the child's identity. At the same time, that identity is reflected in the way the child uses language.

What happens when a couple with two mother tongues use just one language with their child? As the following diagram shows, the child ends up with three active spheres of language use. The result, however, is not as symmetrical as that of a unilingual child growing up in a unilingual environment.

The reason: the child of a mixed couple has the potential for six spheres of language use. By developing only three of them, he or she is missing the other three, which results in a loss of potential.

Diagram 3
Potentially bilingual child
growing up in a unilingual setting

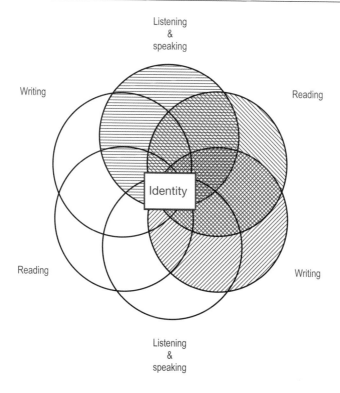

~ 37 ~

As children grow up, their environment expands accordingly. Daycare, preschool, kindergarten or *maternelle*, and school all provide a host of opportunities for them to listen and speak, to read and to write. So does every other aspect of their daily life: the neighbourhood kids (listening and speaking); signs, including billboards, street signs, businesses, etc. (reading); and cards, emails and letters to family and friends (writing).

The increasing variety of language-use opportunities brings with it increasing complexity. For instance, what is the status of French compared with that of English? What is the effect of seeing English on virtually every sign outside of school, and hearing it in stores, government offices and almost everywhere else a child is likely to go? What is the impact of having many sports and leisure activities take place in English? And what about the neighbourhood kids—what influence do they have on our children?

If nothing else, the overwhelming presence of English in our society gives English a status that is hard to match.

In a nutshell...

The children of exogamous couples are born with the potential to develop two mother tongues. If parents decide not to pass on both languages, their kids will end up with a single language. The result will be less satisfying than that of a unilingual child growing up in a unilingual setting, however, because of the loss of potential.

Yo! We's chattin'... 'bout chattin'!

Editor's note: The author has been informed that the above title is entirely inappropriate for this publication. Unfortunately, he has refused to change it. Please accept our humble apologies on his behalf.

Chatting isn't what it used to be. A long, long time ago (say, way back at the end of the last millennium), "chat" was something people did orally, whether in person or on the phone. Nowadays, though, our kids chat without uttering a word, via computer. And it's not just English-speaking kids who do it: francophones use the same word to describe this form of communication.

Now, here's the question: is it wrong for francophone teens (and preteens, and proteins) to use *chat* instead of the "official" word *clavarder*? Our esteemed editor (who, for some reason, objected rather vigorously to the title of this section) would say so, but we know very few francophone youths who would agree.

J'CLAVARDAIS PAS, M'DAME. J'FAISAIS DU **CHATTING** !

This section is all about the many ways we use language. For instance, this book is written in what could be called Standard English, just as the language children learn and use in a francophone school could be labelled Standard French. Some people (*hello, esteemed editor*) consider these the only "acceptable" levels of language.

Yet how many of us use "standard" language all the time? Whether relaxing at home with family, enjoying leisure activities with friends or discussing work with colleagues, we use different words, expressions and sentence structures to reflect the situation, mood, activity, etc. Such variety adds nuance and colours to our language palette. Usually, the variations we use are appropriate to the context—even if they aren't "standard."

This kind of juggling is commonplace among people who speak one language. Just imagine the possibilities when someone has two or more languages to play with!

You've no doubt heard of *franglais*, a blend of French and English. Your children probably use it when they talk or chat with their friends.

> We could say that although *franglais* is a language all its own, it isn't actually its own language. It is, however, a variety of French that many francophone kids use, especially when their parents and teachers aren't listening.

Whether or not we approve, *franglais* is one element of a whole range of language possibilities our children use every day.

It's interesting to note that, although it combines elements of both languages, *franglais* is a variety more of French than of English. And its use is in no way limited to young francophones and Acadians living in a predominantly English-speaking Canadian setting. Just pop by Paris, France, and you'll hear all sorts of English words rolling off purely French tongues. Of course, those Parisians aren't speaking *franglais*… but where does one draw the line?

You'll notice the same phenomenon in the French-speaking regions of New Brunswick and Ontario, and throughout the province of Quebec. Accents may change, expressions may differ, but the use of English words by French speakers isn't limited to francophones living in a minority situation. Whether it's the latest in street chic or just plain laziness is in the ear of the listener. Again, where does one draw the line?

> Francophone parents can start by serving as an example for their children. This doesn't mean constantly correcting them, but rather using French words and expressions instead of the English equivalents.

It can be helpful to repeat something that a young person says, using the French words, though we wouldn't suggest doing this all the time.

Finally, rather than trying to ban language varieties we dislike, our challenge as parents is to teach our kids what is and what isn't appropriate in different situations.

Language use

My child's language use today

The following diagram illustrates several spheres of a child's life. Your mission, should you decide to accept it, is to identify the language(s) or varieties of language your child uses in different situations and relationships. By tallying up the totals, you should have a fairly good idea of how often he or she speaks French, English, *franglais*, another language, or a combination of two or more of the above.

Please write down every variety of language your child is likely to use in a given context; whether or not you approve is another matter.

Diagram 4
Language(s) my child speaks with these people or in these areas of activity:

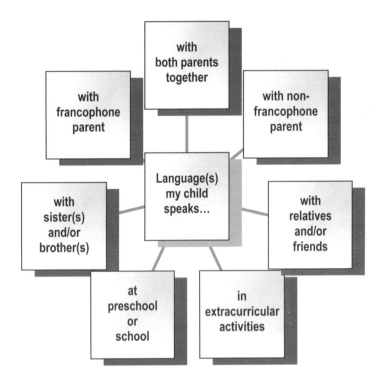

This exercise can become quite complicated depending on your family's language situation—say, if you live closer to one extended family than the other, or if your child speaks more than one language in certain relationships or activities.

Perhaps drawing up a table with three columns would help. That's what you'll find on the next page...

Language(s) my child speaks...

Relationship or activity	Language spoken	Frequency of contact/activity
francophone parent		
non-francophone parent		
both parents together		
sister/brother		
sister/brother		
relative		
relative		
relative		
relative		
relative		
friend		
friend		
friend		
friend		
friend		
preschool/school		
activity		
activity		
activity		
activity		

The results can tell you much about your child's language use today. How does that compare with the following?

My child's language use tomorrow

Repeat the exercise you've just done, but this time take a look into the future, to the time when your child is an adult. What language(s) do you hope he or she will use in each of the following relationships or situations?

Diagram 5
Language(s) I hope my child will speak
with these people or in these areas of activity:

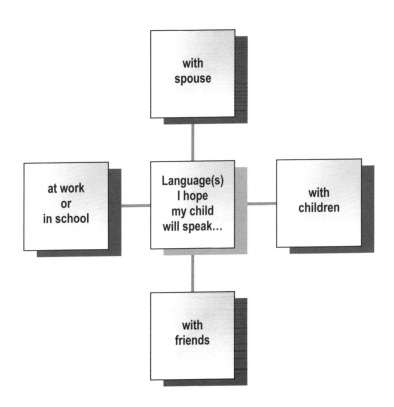

How do the results compare with those you obtained in the first exercise? If your child's current language use continues, will she or he be using language the way you hope in the future? If not, are there any changes you and your spouse can make today?

In a nutshell...

The way our children use language says a lot about them—and about how we're raising them. The decisions we make when they're young, and the example that each parent provides, combine to help young people develop long-lasting language habits.

Language, intelligence and literacy

As every parent knows, and as we saw at the beginning of this chapter, children learn a huge amount before they even set foot in a preschool. During their toddling years, youngsters begin to develop all sorts of things, including their creativity and decision-making abilities; a spirit of initiative, independence and self-confidence; a cultural identity; and the ability to understand and relate to their surroundings.

They also start learning how to learn—a process that can take a variety of forms.

It's hard to overstate the importance of children's early years. Among other things, this is when they start to make sense of the world around them through language, which enables them to understand others and make themselves understood. Children build much of their language foundation before the age of six.

> Preschoolers develop not only vocabulary and grammar, but more complex and abstract language skills too. From using simple words to express their most basic needs, they go on to create imaginary worlds, describe situations and convey information.

Their progress is perhaps most evident on the telephone—especially in conversations with far-away relatives—when they have to rely solely on their ability to use words. Communicating in this way is also central to developing youngsters' reading and writing skills.

As we've seen, children in families with two or more languages have a chance to develop a broad and complex language base. Fortunately, kids are like sponges! They absorb everything that goes through their senses as well as the way it's presented to them. That's why it's so important to create a positive learning atmosphere in the home.

They quickly learn not only to decode their surroundings, but also to code their language use: French with Maman, English with Daddy, Spanish with Abuela and Abuelo...

To the casual observer, this "language juggling" is nothing short of amazing. To the youngsters themselves, well, that's just how they relate to people. The ability to associate languages with individuals is enhanced when parents consistently use their mother tongue with their children. That's the OPOL concept we described in Chapter 2.

> During their early years, children are also busy developing two other key elements of their identity: intelligence and literacy. Infants observe the world around them (often putting much of it into their mouths) and combine all this input to understand their environment.

By closely observing infants' behaviour, parents get an idea of how they perceive their surroundings. This process evolves as the children grow, and over time they become better able to express themselves rather than leaving their parents guessing.

Intelligence and literacy are simple terms but complex notions. For example, some researchers have identified numerous forms of intelligence where others see different components of a single form of intelligence. Regardless of the school of thought, it's clear that intelligence isn't a one-dimensional concept. Nor is literacy, which means much more than knowing how to read and write. Experts now study scientific, mathematical and other forms of literacy that represent a blend (dare we say a *fusion*?) of knowledge, skills and attitudes.

When it comes to children with francophone roots, there are even more dimensions to consider, as we'll see below.

Children with francophone roots

Literacy is central to both academic success and learning throughout a person's life. It's also a concept that has evolved over time: how many parents today would like to be as "computer literate" as their children? Dr. Diana Masny of the University of Ottawa describes literacy this way:

> Literacy is traditionally defined as the ability to read and write. It is usually considered an individual process: each child develops psychological and linguistic elements critical to the acts of reading and writing [...]. Increasingly, however, literacy is defined more broadly and is being viewed as a social phenomenon. Thus, what it means to be literate varies according to socio-cultural groups. The term "literacies" is used in the plural to indicate that an individual can acquire several types of literacy.[6]

Literacy therefore includes cultural skills, behaviours, attitudes and values, and ways of speaking, writing and acting. It has become the focus of extensive research, the basis of government policies, and the object of international studies. Every three years since 2000, for example, the Organisation for Economic Co-operation and Development (OECD) has been measuring the reading, mathematical and scientific literacy of hundreds of thousands of students around the world.[7] In 2006, 57 countries participated. That's a pretty strong statement about the importance of literacy!

---

[6] Diana Masny, "Literacy Development in Young Children." (Canadian Child Care Federation: *Interaction*, Spring 1995).

[7] Programme for International Student Assessment, or PISA.

Children attending French-language schools in a minority setting develop, among others, three fundamental, interrelated literacies: personal, academic and community.[8]

Personal literacy

From the moment they're born, children are surrounded by images, sounds, actions, words—in short, by the world their parents bring them into. As they grow, they learn to decipher all this information, and in the process integrate certain elements that will help shape their individuality.

That's the beginning of what's called personal literacy, or the ability to understand and affirm one's identity. For children of mixed couples, this means learning two or more languages, one of which is French, and understanding and affirming their dual cultural heritage.

MERVEILLEUX, SON! SUPER!

Personal literacy permeates every aspect of a child's life. In many respects, it's the glue that binds together the building blocks of each person's identity. Parents can help their children develop healthy, balanced personal literacy by actively living both languages and cultures.

Academic literacy

This is the traditional form of literacy: the ability to speak, read and write in order to achieve academic success. It entails learning the languages of various disciplines (math, fine arts, science, social studies, language arts, physical education, technology, etc.) that children will study throughout their schooling. It's also the ability to grasp concepts, create links

---

[8] *Affirming Francophone Education — Foundations and Directions: A Framework for French First Language Education in Alberta.* (Edmonton: Alberta Education, French Language Services Branch, 2001), p. 17.

between ideas and, in the case of bilingual children, transfer cognitive skills between languages.

Community literacy

The third form of literacy is the ability to understand and integrate one's community—that is, its ways of thinking, saying, doing and living—as well as society as a whole. For the children of exogamous couples, this means identifying with the minority francophone and majority anglophone communities, and maybe with other language groups too.

Attending a French-language school exposes children not only to an essential component of the local francophone community, but to the regional, national and international Francophonie as well. Outside school, these same children are also in touch with the anglophone community at various levels.

Children's personal and community literacies are reinforced when they have meaningful French-language life experiences in the home, school and community. Taking your child to a French-speaking music teacher, dentist, doctor, or other specialist combines both personal and community literacies. Actions like this confirm the relevance of French in the community and society, which in turn validates the francophone component of your child's identity.

It's important to bring children into contact with the francophone community during their preschool years. As we all know, life BC (before children) bears little resemblance to life AC. Many people find their circle of friends and contacts changing as their circumstances change. One new parent put it this way: "Those late nights out with the 'kidless crowd' lose some of their appeal when you know you can't sleep in the next morning—or *any* morning, for that matter!"

It's not surprising that many parents increasingly find themselves in the company of others with young children. The first step in this direction usually involves finding a daycare, preschool, play group or nursery school. For parents of children with francophone roots, the search for the right establishment means taking into account the francophone component of their identity.

When considering your options, make sure you find childcare workers and educators who not only address your child's physical, intellectual, social, behavioural and emotional needs, but fully understand the implications of her or his dual heritage as well.

In a nutshell...

Literacy is much more than knowing how to read and write. For the children of mixed couples, it means developing personal, academic and community literacies too. It's up to parents to ensure that this development is balanced between the majority and minority languages and cultures.

4. Focus on French

Have you and your francophone spouse discussed, debated, disputed, deliberated and definitively decided to raise your child in both your mother tongues? Do you want him or her to be one of those people who are so comfortable in French and English, and perhaps another language, that they can understand and express themselves as effortlessly as unilingual speakers?

If so, and if you live in a mainly English-speaking region of the country, one of your biggest challenges will be to assure your child's French-language development. That's what this chapter is all about.

First, though, a disclaimer:

> In this chapter, we will shamelessly promote the use of French in your child's life.

Okay, so it won't be the first time. But researchers and teachers and parents and extended families and friends and children have shown and remarked and explained and demonstrated that, in an English setting, the best way for children to become fluent in French is for them to hear, speak, read, write and *live* the language as much as possible.

We're not suggesting you ignore your own language if you're the non-francophone half of your couple! We're just pointing out that it can be a challenge to develop French as a mother tongue (whether alone or as one of two or more mother tongues) in a mainly English-speaking society. If that's what you want for your child, however, there are many ways you can help make it happen.

We'll offer some ideas in the following pages; how you use them is up to you!

Pots o' gold

Researchers sometimes illustrate the relative influence of English and French in a minority setting by drawing a balance that resembles a seesaw or teeter-totter. Now, it just so happens we renewed our poetic licence the other day, so let's put it to use by describing what this research-inspired image is all about...

Imagine your child perched on a seesaw that has a heavy pot of gold at one end. That pot represents the amount of English your child is exposed to from birth until he or she is old enough to vote. The sheer quantity of gold it contains means that your child will be able to understand and speak the language without any problem whatsoever.

Where does all that glittering metal come from? The neighbourhood kids, the soccer league, the stores at the mall… in short, many elements of your child's everyday life.

Your child could slide down the seesaw and latch onto the English pot o' gold or, with your help, he or she could become twice as rich! Here's how: by adding an equal amount of French gold to the other end. Sounds simple: you could, say, simply enrol your little leprechaun in a francophone school and voilà, *instant wealth, right?*

Wrong. While it is an excellent choice, the "Francophone School" pot alone isn't as heavy as that big pot of English gold at the other end. So your child needs more French gold!

What can you do? Hmm... how about adding another pot of gold, this time labelled "Family Life," to the French end? Let's see...

Why, yes, it works! Congratulations, you've now balanced the seesaw—and doubled your child's riches!

The pots o' gold, of course, are the two mother tongues your child can develop, plus all the cultural baggage that accompanies them. In a world where the ability to communicate is one of the most important keys to success, this is true wealth indeed!

Adding French to your child's family life doesn't mean sacrificing English or any other language you or your spouse might speak. Rather, as we saw in the OPOL section, it means the francophone parent always speaks French with the child, and the non-francophone parent actively encourages this practice.

In short, it means ensuring that French is a living, significant language—through play, reading, etc.—and not just something the child uses in the classroom.

Speaking of bilingualism

Most of us agree there are benefits to being bilingual. If you and your spouse have had discussions around raising a bilingual child, you've probably thought of several already. How many can you list offhand?

> Keep in mind that bilingualism is a continuum we could summarize as ranging from "barely" to "fully."

The benefits of bilingualism go beyond what's immediately obvious, too. Whereas a basically bilingual person is able to discuss a limited selection of subjects in two languages, a fully bilingual person will be able not only to discuss more topics, but to communicate with greater precision and nuance.

People with two mother tongues have both the language tools and the cultural references that enable them to understand and communicate fully with others.

People's cultural identity, and their ability to understand and relate to others, necessarily reflects their mother tongue. For instance, Japanese individuals grow up learning the intricacies of Japanese etiquette, which Canadians of non-Japanese origin can grasp only superficially. How many business and political representatives spend hours cramming cultural information into their heads before travelling to Japan, just so they can avoid a social blunder? The same applies to all cultures.

> The children of exogamous couples have the potential to be at the "fully fluent" end of the bilingualism continuum—that is to say, at the point where they fully understand not only language but cultural references as well.

This is a huge advantage that those of us located elsewhere on the continuum can only dream of. Here, for the record, are some benefits of bilingualism:

Social and personal benefits
✓ ability to communicate and maintain relationships with immediate and extended family
✓ potential to create a wide range of friendships and acquaintances
✓ greater sensitivity to others
✓ ability to understand others more fully
✓ enhanced interpersonal skills
✓ greater confidence in social interactions
✓ higher self-esteem
✓ ability to apply appropriate communication skills in different social contexts
✓ deeper and more complex knowledge of cultural specificities
✓ greater flexibility and adaptability in daily life
✓ enhanced tolerance of others
✓ ability to bridge language and cultural boundaries
✓ heightened appreciation of cultural events
✓ ability to understand and appreciate wide variety of humour
✓ possibility to enjoy more rewarding travel experiences.

Cognitive and academic benefits
✓ enhanced academic performance
✓ expanded thinking processes
✓ greater mental versatility
✓ enhanced reasoning skills
✓ better formation of concepts
✓ more flexible thinking habits
✓ better problem-solving and analytical skills
✓ head start in reading because of stronger focus on meaning than on sound
✓ ability to understand texts in their original language
✓ greater awareness of language nuances in different contexts
✓ superior ability to learn other languages
✓ more opportunities to explore different academic options
✓ heightened creativity
✓ stronger conceptual development in two languages
✓ ability to transfer cognitive and academic proficiency between languages
✓ greater collaborative and cooperative learning skills.

Economic and commercial benefits

✓ broader range of communication skills
✓ superior ability to compete in a global economy
✓ increased marketability of skills
✓ greater ability to access essential services
✓ better understanding of other legal and political systems
✓ broader economic prospects.

Benefits of French-English bilingualism

✓ ability to understand and communicate with Canada's two official-language communities
✓ ability to study, work and play anywhere in Canada
✓ potential to study, work and play in countries belonging to the Commonwealth and the Francophonie.

In a nutshell...

The benefits of bilingualism are far more subtle and numerous than one might think, and extend into a variety of spheres. People with two mother tongues have a broader range of abilities, including language and cultural references that help them understand and communicate effectively with others.

Building a framework

What point would you like your child to reach on the bilingualism continuum? If you're aiming for the "fully fluent" end, then your goal will be for her or him to have a solid foundation in both French and your family's other language before she or he becomes an adult.

A simple framework sometimes helps mixed couples reach this goal. Since the present chapter focuses on French, here are some ideas that can help you help your child develop that mother tongue:[9]

Commit

If you're the French-speaking parent, always speak French to your child. If you're the non-French-speaking parent, you can help by actively supporting your spouse and encouraging your child to speak French, too. Without this basic commitment from both parents, it'll be extremely hard to work as a team.

Be consistent

Consistency means encouraging your child to speak French with her or his francophone parent no matter where they are or who else is listening. Bilingualism is something to be proud of and not hidden away! (Remember that these are guidelines, and that some situations call for flexibility. As long as those remain the exception, you'll be well on your way to achieving your goal.)

Correct

When your child makes mistakes in either language, repeat the words or sentences in standard form (though not so often that it becomes discouraging). Teach by example.

---

[9] This section has been adapted from the *Facilitator's Manual* I wrote for the Fédération des parents francophones de Colombie-Britannique's EX Team.

Build

Encourage your child to ask questions, and be sure to answer them. Concepts are easily transferred between languages; make sure your child learns as many new things in French as in your family's other language, so that both are sources of information. Remember, you're striving for balance—but also remember that it's impossible to have too much French in your child's life when he or she is growing up in an English-speaking society.

Reinforce

Surround your child with French music, stories, films, books, games, computer software, and so on. Play family games in French. Build a collection of French rhymes, riddles and sayings your child can use over and over again, because youngsters love repetition!

Use standard language

You and other adults are role models for your child. Discuss all sorts of things with your child (in French if you're the French-speaking parent), and speak your language well. Use standard language in short sentences and encourage your child to speak that way with you. Don't mix your languages unless you want to mix up your child!

Branch out

Show your child that other people speak French, too. She or he needs to hear the language from the many different speakers you'll find in your local francophone community and elsewhere. Make sure your extended francophone family uses only French with your child. Hearing others, especially adults, speak French will help your child build a broader and more solid language base.

Support

Focus on your child's progress in his or her French-language development; you're helping him or her build a foundation for a lifetime of language use.

Have fun

Make sure your child has as much fun in French as he or she does in the other family language!

In a nutshell...

A framework can enable both parents in a mixed couple to help children develop the language skills they need in order to become fully bilingual. Such a framework helps mixed couples work together as a team for the benefit of their children.

Filling the "Family Life" pot

Let's start by stating the obvious, which sometimes becomes less so as our youngsters grow older, but which remains true nonetheless: parents are children's primary educators. That's "primary" as in "first," but also as in "principal, main, chief, most important, key, prime, major and crucial." We gain this lofty status very early in their lives, since at least one parent—and usually both—will be present to welcome a newborn baby into the world.

That, however, is just the beginning...

> We remain a presence in our children's lives long after we cease being a presence on this Earth.

Heavy, eh? Without being overly dramatic, it's true that the decisions we make for our kids, from the moment they're born, help shape their entire lives. Our progeny become who they are, in part, either thanks to us or in spite of us. Here's a quick example: parents in mixed couples can pretty much decide if their children will develop a unilingual or a bilingual identity. How's that for serious influence?

Children of all ages thrive on their parents' encouragement and praise. That's why it's so crucial to demonstrate an active interest in everything they do, from taking their first steps to studying for final exams.

Children at play

As we saw in the section "An a-maze-ing story," children learn a phenomenal amount before they even set foot in a preschool or school. Yet what do they do more than anything else when they're young? Besides sleeping and eating, they play.

If you want to fill the "Family Life" French pot o' gold, here's a good place to start: make sure your children play in French as much as in English or another language. That means when they're babies, toddlers, youngsters, preteens, teens... There's no age limit when it comes to playing, and games that involve problem-solving are particularly beneficial.

> Children will value both parents' languages if they associate them equally with play and other enjoyable activities.

What sorts of games can parents play with their children? Well, what do many parents do with babies? They nibble on fingers and toes. They blow noisily on bellies. They make strange noises and funny faces. In short, they do a lot of things they never thought they'd do!

This is where OPOL (One Parent, One Language) begins. Could anything be more natural for a francophone parent than to play with a baby in French? Or for a Spanish-speaking parent to play in Spanish?

(Sometimes francophone parents say they speak English with their children because their non-francophone spouse suspects they're talking about him or her whenever they speak French. At this point in their children's development, it would be hard to have that reaction, wouldn't it?)

> This is the ideal time to integrate French into your family life, and it's as simple as each of you using your mother tongue whenever you play with your child.

As we mentioned earlier, you and your francophone spouse may always have spoken English together, and this could make him or her feel self-conscious about speaking French to your child, at least in your presence. If you've decided to raise your child in both mother tongues, this is an opportunity to translate words into actions by helping your spouse overcome that awkwardness.

But back to playing: the games you play with your children change as time goes on, but there are always ways to play in French. Here are just a few examples:

On the road

Trips can be trying times for any family. Unless you've got a DVD player in your vehicle and a limitless supply of films your kids will be thrilled to watch over and over again, you're likely to find yourself searching for creative ways to keep your little ones happy on those trips to the cottage or the in-laws'.

A little imagination can turn road trips into fun and memorable family times. These are also excellent opportunities to fill up that French pot of gold, since any game you can invent and play in English can also be played in French. Why don't you try one of the following games on your next trip?

"I spy (with my little eye)..." / "Je vois (avec mes yeux de lynx)..."

⇒ This is one of the oldest road games in the book. It helps children work on their observation and many other skills. It can be played in English, in French or, depending on each family member's language skills, bilingually. Kids who are strong enough in both mother tongues can also translate for unilingual parents.

"I'm thinking of an animal..." / "Je pense à un animal..."

⇒ This is a fun and highly educational game that appeals to kids from the moment they're able to identify certain animals. One person thinks of an animal, and the other passengers have to guess what it is. The participants can ask *oui ou non* questions, and the person with the idea can answer using only one of those two words. As with many games, there's plenty of room for imaginative strategy ("Is it a mammal," etc.). And once again, the game can be played in any language or any combination of languages.

"I'm thinking of a number..." / "Je pense à un chiffre..."

⇒ This is another game in which one person thinks of something—in this case, a numeral between 0 and a number that falls within the children's scope—and the other participants try to find out what it is. It teaches strategy ("Is it between zero and 50, between zero and 25," etc.) as well as numbers themselves. This is an easy game to play in two languages.

"I have..." / "J'ai..."

⇒ This is a "round" game that starts with the letter A. The first player thinks of an object, animal, etc. that starts with the letter A; the second player has to say that word and add something that starts with B, and so on:
> › Player 1: "J'ai une allumette."
> › Player 2: "J'ai une allumette et une banane."
> › Player 3: "J'ai une allumette, une banane et un coussin."

Keep it as simple as need be for everyone to have fun.

These are just four examples of road games families can play in French or in a combination of languages. What are some your family would enjoy?

On the menu

Some families use only one language during certain meals, while others alternate between the family's two mother tongues according to the day or the meal. Much depends on parents' language abilities and willingness to learn (and to make mistakes in front of the kids). Here's one way to incorporate French into a meal: *Pizza à la française*.

Make or buy a crust, then invite the whole family to prepare and add the ingredients they prefer—all in French, of course. It's a delicious way to learn some vocabulary and have fun together.

Making the pizza is the first step in what could become a whole meal during which everyone speaks French. And it's just one idea: there are many meals that families can make together, including stews, soups, sushi...

Whatever course you choose (forgive the pun), meals do provide an excellent opportunity for families to practise their French.

The Sticky Activity

Is this an original idea? I'd like to think so, but other people—including you, perhaps—have no doubt thought of it, too. I first sketched it out in an information sheet for parents whose children attend one of the schools run by the Conseil scolaire Centre-Nord, a francophone school board in Alberta. Then I added flesh to the idea in the Facilitator's Manual I wrote for the group of resource people in British Columbia known collectively as the EX Team. (That's "EX" as in "exogamy," of course.) My goal now is to cover the whole country—literally. Read on and you'll see what I mean...

If your child is learning or already knows how to print, and if you're willing to learn a few words in French and invest some time having educational fun with your child, this game, called "The Sticky Activity," is for you!

➤ *What you'll need*

⇒ a few packs of self-adhesive notes (also called *Post-it* notes or "stickies")
  › a different colour for each player
  › and (if so desired) different shapes
⇒ at least one bilingual dictionary
  › any format, including pocket size
  › visual dictionary a good choice
⇒ pencils and/or pens and/or felt pens

➤ *On your marks...*

Each participant gets his or her own colour (and shape, if you've got a selection) of stickies. *You* get a bilingual dictionary.

Depending on your child's reading abilities, he or she gets either a bilingual dictionary or a human helper—for instance, your francophone spouse or an older sibling. Each participant gets a pen or pencil.

> ## *Get set...*

The *educational* objective is to learn as many words as you can, in French, within a specified time (let's say 30 minutes) for objects around your home. You might want to concentrate on a specific room (for example, the kitchen), or limit yourselves to words that start with a certain letter (such as "A" the first time around).

The *fun* objective is to cover as many objects and surfaces as you can with your stickies!

> ## *Go!*

Print the French word for an object, a surface, a pet, etc. on your sticky, then stick the sticky to the object in question. Whoever has stuck the most stickies around the room or home by the end of the game wins!

Needless to say, the more often you play The Sticky Activity, the more colourful your home will become!

In a nutshell...

The Sticky Activity is just one example of how you and your children can have fun learning French. Ask any child, and you'll know that having fun is one of the best ways to learn a language!

Reading

There's an old saying among teachers: "What we teach children to *want* to do is even more important than what we teach them to *do*." As primary educators, parents have an opportunity—and a responsibility—to cultivate attitudes and abilities that will benefit children all their lives. That's exactly what you do when you sit down and read to your child.

WHEN I GROW UP, I WANT TO PLANT DES FLEURS, MOI AUSSI!

Reading aloud to youngsters has been advocated by experts for decades. It's a simple activity that helps them learn not only to read, but also to listen, speak and write. Most importantly, it helps them develop a positive attitude toward reading, which lies at the heart of education. No matter what avenue children take in life, their reading skills will always serve them well.

Promoting reading is one of the cornerstones of the National Literacy Secretariat (NLS), a Canadian government body that sets national directions for literacy programs. According to the NLS, "When parents read to their children, they show them that the written word is the key to learning and that learning can be fun."[10]

> Language literacy in the home is the foundation for a lifelong love of reading and writing among youngsters. It's also strongly linked to achievement in school and in the workplace.

[10] *Family Literacy in Canada*. (Ottawa: Human Resources Development Canada, 2001).

When should parents read to children?

Is there a "right" time to start reading to children? Well, how many parents start speaking to their offspring before the little bundles of joy pop into the world? Many. So why not start reading to them then as well?

Studies have shown that unborn babies respond to the sound of stories being read to them, just as they respond to each of their parents' voices. Since the intonation and rhythm of reading differ from those we use when we speak, reading to babies before they're born can help attune their ears to the nuances of sound.

Some people think this is silly, but let's face it: parents-to-be do some pretty silly things sometimes!

When your child's a baby...

What a discovery it must be for a baby to see, feel and smell a book—to say nothing of tasting it! What really brings books alive, though, is when parents start to read. All of a sudden, something magical happens: this bland-tasting object has the power to transform adults' voices! And what fun for the parents, who get to make, repeat, alter, exaggerate, and even mangle a multitude of simple sounds.

In many ways, this is an ideal opportunity for non-French-speaking parents who'd like to learn the language, or at least a few words. Some non-francophone parents enjoy reading to their children in French, even if they struggle with certain sounds or structures. It all depends on each person's comfort level.

By the way, we've yet to hear of children suffering from hearing their non-francophone parent read to them in French.

Reading at this stage, regardless of language, involves a lot of repetition as well as rhythm and even some musicality. Just letting your child explore books, using all her or his senses, is a great learning experience in itself. This experimentation is sometimes called "pre-reading."

AND THIS, JE SUPPOSE, IS **YOUR COMFORT LEVEL** FOR READING IN FRENCH ?

As your child grows...

As children grow and their language skills develop, their reading needs also evolve. They progress from simple picture books with few words to stories of increasing complexity and fewer illustrations. All along the way, parents have a role to play regardless of their mother tongue.

➢ *When your child starts to speak*

Books contain more words as children start to build their vocabulary, develop their imagination, extend their attention span and explore their emotions. In addition to reading the words, parents can start asking children to find objects on the page: "Where is the...?" "*Où est le/la...?*" At this stage, youngsters may randomly select pages rather than read from beginning to end. Let them! As long as they're enjoying themselves, they're learning the most important lesson: reading is fun!

➢ *When your child enters preschool, kindergarten and early grades*

Stories become more complex, as do the illustrations. Now, instead of merely finding an object on the page, children start recognizing simple repeated words (*a, and, the, le, la, de, du*). They love to hear the same stories over and over again, and may want to invent stories of their own—even when you're in the middle of reading to them! Their creative juices are starting to flow, and the connection with the written word will stimulate their desire to learn how to write.

➢ *When your child enters higher elementary grades*

When children start learning to read themselves, some parents think it's time to stop reading aloud to them—but it isn't. As they grow older, children become increasingly active listeners by, among other things, learning to form images based on what they hear. It's a very important process that will enable them to grasp difficult concepts later on. Best of all, imaging is a skill they gain from being read to in any language.

Not only should you continue reading aloud, but this is also a good time to introduce children to dictionaries, encyclopedias and websites you can consult together. Bring French books and magazines (as well as English and other languages if relevant to your family) into the home as well, and ensure they're always within easy reach. Make family outings to the local library, museum, science centre, cultural centre, book fair, and so on. While you're at the library, don't hesitate to ask for specific French books and magazines, and encourage the librarians to expand their French section. The more parents express the need for French reading material, the more material they'll find on the shelves!

> ### *When your child enters higher grades*

Teenagers sometimes abandon reading because they equate it solely with schoolwork. If they've been read to since birth and have consistently read themselves, however, this probably won't happen. You can keep your teenagers' interest in reading alive by accompanying them to the library (it makes a good destination when they're learning to drive), buying them publications in fields that interest them (fashion or hockey, for instance) and continuing to set the example by reading yourself.

What can a non-francophone parent do when it comes to reading in French?

Some non-francophone parents are content to read to their children in their mother tongue. Others want to try reading in French as well as, or instead of, their mother tongue. As far as children's language development goes, the OPOL concept applies as much to reading as to all other aspects of language use. Having a non-francophone parent speak and read in French, however, is a bonus.

If that's what you like to do, go for it! Given the strong presence of English in much of the outside world, it's hard to have too much French in your kids' lives.

If you're not comfortable reading aloud in French, why not simply join your francophone spouse when he or she reads to the children? Your very presence shows that you value the language, and you can't help but pick up some vocabulary and grammar in the process. It's a great way not only to participate, but to form lasting family bonds centred on an extremely beneficial activity.

The bottom line is this: reading is one of the most important things you can do with your children, regardless of the language you use. Since we're filling the "Family Life" pot here, however, we'd encourage you and your spouse to take every possible opportunity to read to your child in French—he or she will benefit from it for an entire lifetime.

In a nutshell...

Reading to children is by far one of the most important activities parents can do. It's essential that the francophone parent read in French; the non-francophone parent can do likewise, if he or she is comfortable, or accompany the francophone parent at story time. Helping children learn to read is to help them develop an essential lifelong skill.

Tips for non-francophone parents

If you want to read to your children in French:
⇒ Start when they're young.
⇒ Ask your spouse for help with vocabulary and pronunciation.
⇒ Have fun when you read, even with hard-to-pronounce French sounds.
⇒ Read to your children in French for as long as you feel comfortable, then...
⇒ ... read to them in English.
⇒ Consult French-language dictionaries, encyclopedias and websites with your children.
⇒ Join your francophone spouse when she or he reads to the children in French.
⇒ Bring French books and magazines into your home, and make sure reading material is always within easy reach.
⇒ Join and regularly visit your local French-language resource centre.
⇒ Contact your local, provincial or territorial francophone associations for information on obtaining French-language books and magazines.
⇒ Encourage municipal and regional libraries to expand their French section.
⇒ Accompany your teens to the library.
⇒ Buy French publications in your children's fields of interest.
⇒ Set the example by reading yourself.

Tips for francophone parents

If your spouse wants to read to your children in French:
⇒ Be patient!
⇒ Encourage him or her to start as early as possible.
⇒ Help with vocabulary by explaining or translating.
⇒ Help with pronunciation.
⇒ Set the example by reading in French yourself.

Topping up the pot

Playing and reading provide countless opportunities to fill up the French "Family Life" pot. There are many other things you can do, too, including the following:

Make French the official language of certain rooms, or during specific activities.

Listen to French music or stories whenever you're driving to and from preschool or school.

Dedicate Friday evenings to watching family movies in French (complete with a bowl of popcorn—er, *maïs soufflé*).

Listen to French radio stations and watch French-language television programming.

Listen to French-language music (every province and territory is home to fantastic musicians who record in French).

Hire French-speaking babysitters.

Play board and card games in French.

Obtain electronic games in French (you can usually choose the language).

Tell your kids how proud you are that they know French.

If you haven't done so yet, invest in a DVD player, since DVDs usually allow you to select the language you watch a movie in.

Join and regularly visit your local French-language resource centre, where you'll find items such as books, videos, DVDs and games.

Make it a habit for the French-speaking parent in your couple always to speak French with your children.

If you aren't a francophone, speak the standard form of your own mother tongue to your children—but, depending on your family's situation and your French-language abilities, don't hesitate to speak to them in French.

In a nutshell...

There's virtually no limit to the number of ways you can help fill your children's French "Family Life" pot. You have opportunities every single day, from the time they're babies, to help them learn French. Whether playing with them, or taking part in everyday activities, or reading, you and your spouse can always find ways to ensure that your children develop French as a mother tongue.

5. Education

Mixed couples in Canada are a lucky lot for many reasons, including the fact that they have more options for their children's schooling. That includes francophones outside Quebec and anglophones who reside in *la belle province*.

When you and your spouse consider your options, it's important to understand what each form of education is intended to do. For example, do you know the differences between a French-language education and a French immersion program?

There are fundamental differences between the two, just as there are between immersion and "core" or "basic" French. The three types of schooling serve three different purposes. Parents' choices depend on their options, priorities, goals—and Charter rights.

French-language education

French-language (also called French first-language or francophone) education is tailor-made for children with francophone roots. Its mandate is "to ensure that students receive a good education in all subjects and disciplines. French-language schools also have a mandate to protect, enhance, and transmit the French language and culture."[11] To that end, the francophone school is "a facility designed for living, learning, and integrating the French language, culture and community."[12]

In other words, the French-language school exists not only to address students' academic needs, but to help them explore and develop their francophone heritage. The emphasis on learning in French, when combined with a living French family life, also enables them to reach a high level of bilingualism.

French first-language education is intended for children who are eligible under section 23 of the Canadian Charter of Rights and Freedoms. Francophone schooling takes place entirely in French from kindergarten to the end of high school. Ideally, French language and francophone culture in the classroom are a natural extension of the children's family and community life. Students also learn the English Language Arts curriculum.

> Upon graduation, students can expect to be highly proficient in French, identify with francophone culture, and have a sense of belonging to the francophone community. They'll also be highly proficient in English, and be able to pursue postsecondary studies and work in either official language.

---

[11] Aménagement linguistique — A Policy for Ontario's French-Language Schools and Francophone Community. (Toronto: Ontario Ministry of Education, 2004), p. 5.
[12] *Affirming Francophone Education*, p. 9.

French immersion

French immersion is designed for children who don't have francophone family roots. The goal in an immersion program is to learn French as a second language. French is the language of instruction for a significant portion of each school day, although the amount varies from one program to another. Immersion begins with a focus on language acquisition so that students can learn to speak and read French well enough to study other subjects in that language. They also take the English Language Arts curriculum and other courses in English.

> When they complete an immersion program, students can expect to be functionally fluent in French (able to live, work and pursue postsecondary studies in French). In addition, they'll have gained an understanding and appreciation of francophone culture.

Core French

Like immersion, "core French" or "basic French" instruction is designed for children heritage other than program, however, a subject, like math, English and science. the classroom as the communication, and their knowledge and different themes or

with a family French. In this French is taught as social studies, French is used in main language of students develop abilities through projects.

> Upon completing a core French program, students can expect to have a good basis in French from which to pursue fluency. They'll also have gained insights into, and an appreciation of, francophone culture.

Both immersion and core programs provide students with the opportunity to learn French as a second language, with all the inherent benefits in Canada and on the international scene. Many educators, business leaders and legislators favour the learning of more than one language, and it's a requirement in numerous postsecondary institutions. A strong advocate of second-language teaching is the Humanities and Social Sciences Federation of Canada, which notes that the European Union is already moving toward a minimum three-language standard for students in its member countries.[13]

Children who receive any of the three types of French education will be able to appreciate other languages, cultures and communities throughout Canada and around the world. Their horizons truly will be broadened by the experience, no matter which path they have taken.

In a nutshell...

French-language education is intended for children with a francophone family heritage; enrolment in a francophone school is a right under section 23 of the Charter of Rights and Freedoms. French immersion and core French programs, on the other hand, are designed to teach non-francophone children French as a second language. The three types of French education are geared to three distinct sets of outcomes.

---

[13] *Policy and Advocacy Perspectives, Special Congress Issue.* (Humanities and Social Sciences Federation of Canada, 2001).

Tips for parents

⇒ Visit your local francophone, immersion and anglophone schools.

⇒ Ask to sit in on francophone, immersion and core French classes.

⇒ Meet with counsellors from the different schools and school boards to discuss your child's situation, bearing in mind that counsellors in French-language institutions generally have a more complete understanding of the issues facing mixed couples and their children.

⇒ Contact your provincial or territorial francophone parent association.

⇒ Discuss your options openly with each other.

⇒ Understand the implications of each type of French education.

⇒ Always keep in mind this question: "What's best for our child?"

Section 23

Parents who enrol their children in a francophone school have several things in common, not the least of which is a constitutional right. These "rights holders" qualify under section 23 of the Canadian Charter of Rights and Freedoms, which applies to anglophone residents of Quebec and francophones who live elsewhere in Canada.

In the territories and provinces outside Quebec, section 23 can be summarized this way:

> The following parents have the right to have their children educated in a francophone school:
>
> 1. Canadian citizens whose first language learned and still understood is French;
>
> 2. Canadian citizens who received their primary school instruction in Canada in French;
>
> 3. Canadian citizens of whom any child has received or is receiving primary or secondary school instruction in French in Canada.

The "school instruction in French" we're referring to here doesn't include instruction received in a French immersion program. The reason, as you'll already know if you've read the previous section, is this: immersion isn't intended for francophones, but rather for non-francophone students who learn French as a second language. Its mandate and goals are different from that of a francophone school, because it's intended for a different clientele.

Many people believe that children are rights holders under section 23, but it's actually their parents who hold the title. Yet when the parents exercise that right, they do so for the benefit of their kids.

Who exactly does this include?

Outside the province of Quebec, section 23 applies first of all to francophones—that is to say, people who speak French because it's their mother tongue. They may have been born in Hamilton or Halifax, White Rock or Winnipeg, or anywhere else in Canada (or in another country, provided they're now Canadian citizens). Whether they're part of a francophone couple or an exogamous couple in no way affects their status as rights holders.

> Non-francophone parents in mixed couples gain section 23 rights themselves when their children attend a francophone school, since they then satisfy the third criterion.

The second category of rights holders includes Canadian citizens who aren't necessarily francophone by birth but who attended a French primary school. This would be the case, for example, of an anglophone couple living in Sherbrooke in 1974 who decide to send their daughter to a French primary school. The girl grows up, marries another anglophone and, in 2007, moves to Barrie, Ontario. Since she satisfies the second criterion of section 23, she has the right to offer her own children the same chance she had to learn French and integrate into Franco-Canadian culture.

The third category applies to parents of children whose sister or brother attends or has attended a French primary, junior high or senior high school in Canada. This includes blended families or those that move to a predominantly English-speaking province or territory after the older children have already begun their schooling in French. By enrolling them in a francophone school, the parents can ensure that those children continue their French-language education, and that all their children receive a similar education.

> Not all section 23 rights holders understand or speak French, yet they all have the same right to enrol their children in a francophone school.

When section 23 parents exercise the right to enrol their youngsters in a francophone school, they effectively pass on the right to their children. Parents who choose English-language or immersion schooling, however, eliminate their children's eligibility under the second criterion. Francophone parents who don't pass on French to their children as a mother tongue eliminate the first criterion.

Each new section 23 parent has the choice of whether or not to pass on the status of "rights holder" to her or his children. It's an individual choice (or, preferably, a decision made by the couple) with far-reaching implications because if the right isn't renewed by each generation, it risks disappearing.

Who else can enrol their children?

Section 23 rights holders make up the vast majority of francophone school communities across the country. However, some governments and school authorities interpret the Charter more generously by allowing certain other parents to enrol their children in the French-language school system.

For instance, there are people who have francophone roots but who, for various reasons, don't speak French—such as the fact that there were no francophone schools where they grew up. These parents may wish to reintegrate their family's original mother tongue into their children's lives, and some school authorities will offer them that possibility.

Other parents who may sometimes enrol their children in francophone schools are non-Canadian citizens who come from countries where French is an official language, like Haiti or Rwanda. A few other exceptional cases may also be permitted with the approval of an administrator or a committee.

The roots of section 23

National charters are usually written in general terms that identify and guarantee fundamental, universal rights. In this context, section 23 of the Canadian Charter of Rights and Freedoms is quite unique, since it applies specifically to the members of Canada's two official-language minorities. It also grants an individual right that has a direct, significant impact on entire communities.

Before the Charter was adopted (and for a number of years afterwards), the education system put francophones at a disadvantage. There were several reasons for this, including the fact that members of the English-speaking majority could neither fully understand francophones' needs nor meet those needs within the existing school system.

> The lack of access to an appropriate education caused many francophone families to lose their ties to the French language and culture. As a result, francophone communities lost the members they needed in order to survive and grow. They also lost their capacity to serve these people in their mother tongue, thereby creating a vicious circle of dwindling numbers and decreasing services.

This had been going on for a long time in most parts of Canada when the Charter was adopted in 1982.

The authors of the Charter knew what was happening and wanted to rectify the situation. They understood that language and culture both play a vital role in the development of a person's identity and in the health of communities. They also knew how important schools are when it comes to passing along language and culture to young people.

Their solution was to grant members of the two official-language minorities a right that, once exercised, would reinforce their communities. The authors went even further by excluding section 23 from the "notwithstanding" clause, which meant that every provincial and territorial government was obliged to respect and apply this federal law.

The fruit of section 23

If you're a rights holder and decide to send your children to a francophone school, you offer them a chance not only to learn the curriculum of your province or territory in French, but to immerse themselves in francophone culture as well. If your kids remain in the francophone system, they'll master French and identify themselves as francophones. This doesn't mean they won't see themselves as anglophones, too, if their other parent (you, perhaps?) is an anglophone, or as members of any other cultural group if you and your spouse have other roots and share them with your children.

> By enrolling your youngsters in a French-language school, you're also contributing to the growth of the francophone community locally as well as provincially and nationally. In other words, you're part of a vast social initiative whose results will be seen in one, two, three or four generations.

Section 23 is thus both an individual right and a community asset. For your children, however, it's much more than that: it's a key that will open countless doors to personal development, educational opportunities and professional advancement. When you exercise your right to a French-language education, you're really giving your children a gift they'll benefit from all their lives!

Are you a parent with francophone roots?

If you have francophone roots but speak little or no French, the decision to enrol your child in a French-language school is particularly significant. Many francophone families across the country lost their French-speaking identity before the Charter came into effect, and some lost it afterward, too.

By reintegrating the language into your family, you'll be setting things right—and that's no small feat! In fact, this could prove to be as much a rewarding personal journey for you as an educational experience for your child.

Enrolling your child in a francophone school shows that French is important—for your child, that is.

In order to be consistent, shouldn't you show that the language is important for you, too? Otherwise, it won't be long before your youngster notices that she or he is the only one carrying the French family torch. And that just might create some doubts...

Here are a few things you can do:

⇒ Dig out the old family photo albums, learn as much as you can about your family history, and share all this information with your child.

⇒ Contact and visit French-speaking relatives to show your child that French is a living fact in your family.

⇒ Enrol in French courses.

⇒ Try speaking French with your child—and don't be afraid to make mistakes! The message you convey, that French is important to you, will have a far greater impact than a few minor deviations from Standard French.

⇒ Introduce French into your family life; try some of the ideas you'll find in Chapter 4.

⇒ Speak French whenever you visit your child's school.

⇒ Attend francophone community events with your family.

What is section 23 intended to do?

Section 23 of the Charter is intended to help protect Canada's two official languages by providing minority groups of both languages with education in their mother tongue, thereby enhancing the vitality of their communities. In its 1990 Mahé decision, the Supreme Court ruled that legislators had given section 23 a three-part role in protecting the language and culture of the country's linguistic minorities:

⇒ **Flourishing of Canada's two official languages**
First, the general purpose of section 23 is "to preserve and promote the two official languages of Canada, and their respective cultures, by ensuring that each language flourishes, as far as possible, in provinces where it is not spoken by the majority of the population." (Judgment, p. 13)

⇒ **Correcting the erosion of minorities**
Section 23 is also intended "to correct, on a national scale, the progressive erosion of minority official language groups and to give effect to the concept of 'equal partnership' of the two official language groups in the context of education." (Judgment, p. 15)

⇒ **Creating major institutional structures**
Finally, section 23 introduces a new kind of guarantee. In order to be effective, it "confers upon a group a right which places positive obligations on government to alter or develop major institutional

structures." (Judgment, p. 16) The francophone school board is one example of a major institutional structure.

Section 23 has a direct impact on individuals and families, but it also has far-reaching implications for francophone communities from the local to the national level.

In a nutshell...

Eligibility under section 23 of the Canadian Charter of Rights and Freedoms determines who can enrol their child in a francophone school. This individual right plays a central role in a long-term, nation-wide endeavour to protect and promote Canada's two official languages.

A brief history of French-language education

French-language schools aren't exactly what you'd call a fixture on the Canadian landscape. In fact, until recently, francophones outside Quebec had very few opportunities to be educated in their mother tongue, let alone govern their own institutions. That's because most provinces and territories had a restrictive—and, in some cases, downright hostile—attitude toward French-language education within their borders.

> There's no such thing as "the good old days" when it comes to francophone education!

Then along came the Constitution Act, 1982, which included the Canadian Charter of Rights and Freedoms and its constitutional guarantees for minority-language education rights. Section 23 of the Charter made the provinces and territories responsible for providing primary and secondary schooling to their official-language minorities in their mother tongue wherever numbers warranted.

> Section 23 was intended to address the educational needs of anglophones in Quebec and Franco-Canadians in every other region of Canada.

One of its goals was to strengthen the vitality of the English-language community in Quebec and French-language communities elsewhere. As Victor Goldbloom, former Commissioner of Official Languages, observed:

> Few can doubt the importance of minority language schools to the vitality of their communities. Such institutions provide an essential physical and social space within which members can meet and foster their cultural and linguistic heritage. Indeed, without minority language schools, the very conditions necessary for the preservation of Canada's linguistic duality would be markedly diminished.[14]

The Charter explicitly stated that the "notwithstanding clause" did not apply to section 23. This meant that provincial and territorial governments had a legal obligation, and a constitutional responsibility, to provide schooling to the official-language minorities in their mother tongue.

> Despite the strong constitutional guarantee, francophone schools didn't sprout up across the country overnight. The provinces and territories chose instead to drag their feet—and found themselves dragged straight into court by groups of parents demanding that their rights be respected.

---

[14] *School Governance: The Implementation of Section 23 of the Charter.* (Ottawa: Office of the Commissioner of Official Languages, 1998).

One of the problems was that anglophone school boards understandably focused on meeting the needs of the majority. No matter how well-intentioned they might be, they simply couldn't fully grasp or address the aspirations of the official-language minority. As a result, francophones were denied programs, services, funding and facilities. In short, their constitutional rights were not being respected.

Every year that governments put off implementing section 23 of the Charter, more children lost touch with their francophone heritage.

Families and communities paid a heavy price for the short-term vision of politicians who refused to respect their rights.

> As they say in French, *plus ça change*—the more things change, the more they stay the same. There are valuable lessons in those francophones' experience that should not be lost on anyone today.

Francophones took various governments to court starting in 1983, and won some 20 court rulings over the next two decades. One of the most significant was the landmark 1990 Mahé v. Alberta case, where the Supreme Court ruled that Canada's official-language minorities had the constitutional right not only to be educated in their mother tongue, but also to govern their own educational institutions.

Other key decisions included the Reference re Public Schools Act (Manitoba) in 1993, Arsenault-Cameron v. Prince Edward Island in 2000, and Doucet-Boudreau v. Nova Scotia (Minister of Education) in 2003.

> After all the years of struggle, francophone education is still in its early stages.

There are countless issues to deal with in any project of this scale, from the grassroots level up to the national political scene. For example, francophone school boards strive to offer students an education that's equivalent to that provided by anglophone institutions, but the French-language boards often lack the necessary resources. How long the struggle for equivalence will last is anyone's guess.

One of the more pressing challenges today involves bringing together both francophone and non-francophone parents in a structure that exists to serve the needs of the francophone community.

In a nutshell...

Minority francophone education is a recent phenomenon across Canada: in many regions, it represents the first real opportunity for francophones to be educated in their mother tongue. The 1982 Canadian Charter of Rights and Freedoms, along with numerous court rulings, have provided minority-language communities with the tools they long needed to overcome generations of assimilation, let alone flourish.

The French-language school

The main goal of any school system is to provide students with the educational experiences they need to ensure their intellectual, emotional and social development. Minority-language schools are no exception. However, they also have a complementary, twofold objective: to develop, maintain and enhance students' French-language skills and culture, and to contribute to the vitality of the francophone community. In concrete terms, this means enriching students' learning with relevant cultural references.[15]

Francophone education must satisfy not only the text but also the intent of the Canadian Charter of Rights and Freedoms, as interpreted in various Supreme Court rulings such as Mahé and Arsenault-Cameron. To that end, it must be a linguistic, cultural and community-based initiative that, among other things:

⇒ affirms children's identity and sense of belonging to the francophone community,

⇒ counters linguistic and cultural assimilation, and

⇒ leads to the creation of francophone schools and school boards.

It would be a mistake to suggest that the learning of French alone satisfies the intent of either the Charter or various court decisions. "Underlying every linguistic enterprise is a deeper cultural motivation. If such enterprises are not built on a solid foundation rich with cultural experience that heightens the sense of belonging and identity, they risk collapsing much faster than they were erected."[16]

More than just four walls

Under section 23 of the Charter, French-language schools and school boards are institutional structures that enable parents to

---

[15] Michael O'Keefe, *Francophone Minorities: Assimilation and Community Vitality*, 2nd edition. (Ottawa: Department of Canadian Heritage, 2001), p. 75.

[16] Benoît Cazabon, *L'aménagement linguistique : le cas de la francisation*. (Éducation et Francophonie, Vol. XX, No. 2, August 1992).

exercise their rights. The francophone school is much more than four walls. Rather, it...

⇒ is a place of learning devoted to the academic success, lifelong learning, and personal growth of all its students.

⇒ contributes to the building of students' cultural identity through the development of their knowledge and use of the French language, as well as a profound sense of the cultural and universal values shared by francophone communities here and elsewhere.

⇒ fosters quality instruction by working with its school board and teaching staff.

⇒ consolidates and expands its educational and cultural network through school-community projects and various partnerships.[17]

Francophone schools aren't intended solely for students, either. According to the Supreme Court of Canada, they "provide community centres where the promotion and preservation of minority language culture can occur; they provide needed locations where the minority community can meet and facilities which they can use to express their culture."[18]

Given its multi-faceted *raison d'être*, the French-language school can be described as an educational and community facility built on the pillars of language, identity, culture and community integration.

---

[17] *Aménagement linguistique*, p. 5.

[18] *Mahé v. Alberta*, [1990] 1 S.C.R. at 363.

Mandate and goals

Francophone education has a dual mandate: to provide instruction based on francophone language, culture and community, and to help correct individual and collective assimilation.

To accomplish this, teachers enrich their classroom instruction with cultural and community experiences. Students not only learn the curriculum of their province or territory, but also gain a sense of belonging to the local, national and international francophone community.

The school's mandate translates into several specific goals:

1. *Students gain the knowledge, skills and attitudes prescribed in their provincial or territorial curriculum.*

    They do this by...
    - ⇒ exploring and developing their intellectual, emotional and social potential
    - ⇒ receiving quality instruction in all subjects
    - ⇒ developing an appreciation and respect for the bilingual character and multicultural nature of Canada.

---

2. *Students integrate the French language, and identify with francophone culture and the francophone community.*

    They do this by...
    - ⇒ mastering French as a mother tongue
    - ⇒ awakening and strengthening their francophone cultural identity
    - ⇒ developing a sense of belonging to the local, national and international francophone community
    - ⇒ gaining solid knowledge of French-Canadian history and of the Francophonie in general
    - ⇒ learning to appreciate the multiethnic and culturally diverse nature of the francophone community.

---

3. **Students acquire a solid knowledge of English.**

They do this by...

⇒ mastering English through balanced French-English bilingualism

⇒ appreciating and understanding anglophone culture locally, nationally and globally

⇒ participating fully in society as bilingual citizens.

4. *The school serves as a focal point of French language and culture for students, families and the larger francophone community.*

This is done this by...

⇒ opening the school's doors to parents and the francophone community

⇒ fostering creativity and encouraging students to participate in francophone community activities

⇒ promoting partnerships in order to strengthen ties between school, family and community, and to ensure the authenticity and relevance of francophone education

⇒ recognizing and valuing different language levels and cultural diversity within the francophone community.

WHAT ABOUT TAKING LES ENFANTS TO SEE THAT FRENCH PLAY?

ON POURRAIT Y ALLER À BICYCLETTE!

STAYING IN SHAPE WHILE HELPING TO SHAPE THEIR CHILDREN'S EDUCATION...!

By understanding the francophone school's mandate and goals, parents can help shape their children's education.

"What was that about kids learning English?"

Caught your attention with that third point, did we? "Students acquire a solid knowledge of English." This sounds good to many parents, both francophone and non-francophone, since the mastery of English is one of the most common concerns of couples whose children attend a French-language school.

English-speaking parents want their children to explore and develop their anglophone roots. French-speaking parents want their children to be able to flourish in an English setting without compromising their French. It's only natural to wonder whether children's home and school life will enable them to become fluent in both parents' mother tongues:

> *"If we send our kids to a francophone school, and keep them there until they graduate, will their English be good enough for them to work or study in English?"*

The answer is a resounding *Yes!* Scientific research consistently shows that learning a minority language can actually enhance both the minority and majority languages. An expert in the field of bilingualism, Dr. Jim Cummins of the University of Toronto, explains the "linguistic interdependence principle" this way:

> [...] although the surface aspects of different languages (e.g. pronunciation, fluency, etc.) are clearly separate, there is an underlying cognitive/academic proficiency that is common across languages. This "common underlying proficiency" makes possible the transfer of cognitive/academic or literacy-related skills across languages.[19]

Cummins also notes that students reap the greatest benefits from bilingualism when their reading and writing skills in both languages are fully developed.

---

[19] Jim Cummins, "Immersion Education for the Millennium: What We Have Learned from 30 Years of Research on Second Language Immersion". (Ontario Institute for Studies in Education of the University of Toronto, 2000).

Students' mastery of English depends on the nature, intensity and frequency of their contacts with the language. In exogamous households, those contacts pose no difficulty whatsoever. Here's what you can expect to see if your child is fluent in French when he or she starts school:

⇒ In Grade 3, francophone students' English-language skills tend to be weaker than those of unilingual anglophone children. The reason: most French-language schools concentrate on building a solid foundation in French before they introduce English, which usually happens in or after Grade 3.

⇒ By Grade 6, however, students in French-language schools have usually caught up.

⇒ By Grade 9, they often perform as well as or better than their unilingual counterparts.

⇒ By the end of high school, they'll have strong enough skills in both English and French that they can live, work and study anywhere in either language.

The francophone educational project

French-language schools often come into being thanks to lobbying by a group of parents. In the not-so-distant past, their words usually fell on deaf ears. Even though matters have improved recently, the process still involves many people and a lot of hard work.

> Awareness-raising and lobbying are the start of what's sometimes called the francophone educational project. This can be defined as "a concept and a framework for supporting and fostering the development, implementation and renewal of the francophone school and its programming."[20]

---

[20] *Affirming Francophone Education*, p. 27.

Opening a school is just the first step in the educational project. In fact, the work is far from over: the educational and cultural needs of students, families and the francophone community must constantly be monitored and met. It's an ongoing, collaborative effort that requires dialogue and tangible commitments in the classroom, the home and the community.

The home-school-community partnership is central to the success of any educational project.

In a nutshell...

French-language education is intended to meet students' educational and cultural needs, and to enhance the vitality of the francophone community. Its goals include teaching students the curriculum of their province or territory; helping them identify with the francophone language, culture and community; enabling them to master English; and providing a focal point of French language and culture for students, families and the extended francophone community. A French-language school's success depends on the participation of families, the school and the community in its educational project.

The home-school-community partnership

Mixed couples who choose a French-language daycare, pre-school, kindergarten or school for their children become part of a community that can understand them better than any other. Such institutions exist to fill a need among francophone and exogamous couples for services tailored to their situation. By assisting these families, they also serve the minority community. The result: children find themselves at the heart of a three-way educational partnership that supports them from their preschool years until the day they graduate from high school.

The home-school-community partnership makes children's education meaningful. Parents play a central role at home as primary educators, addressing their children's diverse needs and helping them develop the various components of their identity.

The school helps children develop different forms of literacy by teaching the provincial or territorial curriculum, which aims at forming educated, well-rounded citizens. In French-language schools, there's also a focus on the specific needs of children with a francophone heritage. Finally, the community provides real-life experiences through activities and services that validate children's home and school education.

But what exactly is that community? It's seldom an area we can physically identify, like a specific neighbourhood or region. Rather, it's made up of people who share French language and culture but who may live far apart. Even in a city like Vancouver, which is home to some 30,000 francophones, getting together can be a challenge because of traffic and other logistical obstacles. That's one reason the French-language school is so valuable when it comes to bringing the language and culture alive for children.

Francophone communities have much to offer those who wish to participate. From sports to business to quilting to politics, there are as many avenues to explore as there are fields of interest. Then there are the special occasions, such as a corn roast or *cabane à sucre*, when everyone in the community joins together for a big party.

Francophone associations may also invite, alone or with partners such as music societies or the Alliance française, French-speaking musicians from across Canada or abroad for concerts and workshops. They may hold annual film festivals, summer festivals or winter carnivals. Maybe there's a local French-language theatre society that welcomes budding actors. For infants, there might be a francophone play group; for adults, lectures or courses in conversational French, wine tasting, history… The possibilities are endless!

The community also plays an educational role that goes beyond festivals and other cultural events. For example, teachers can expand the scope of class projects by having students visit French-speaking professionals, interview francophone residents and meet with government officials. This kind of innovative approach to learning broadens students' horizons by providing meaningful French-language experiences outside the school setting.

All these cultural and educational activities provide valuable opportunities to use French outside the home and school, and to meet other French-speaking people. They also let youngsters see that francophones can be found in places other than the desk next to theirs.

To help your child develop the francophone component of his or her identity, consider supporting and participating in your local francophone community. Join a French-language club that interests you, enrol your youngsters in a sport they enjoy, attend French church services, participate in cultural events! The entire family will benefit from the experience.

You can also promote the use of French in society as a whole. We've already seen an example in the Reading section, where parents can encourage their local library to stock more French-language books and magazines. There are always opportunities to take similar actions elsewhere. For instance, if you deal with a company that's supposed to serve Canadians in both languages (such as an airline) or with the federal government (or the provincial government in New Brunswick) and you notice that service is provided in English only, just think of your francophone spouse. Would he or she appreciate this snub? Not likely. So why not mention it to the appropriate authority in person, on the phone, by letter or in an email? It's this kind of action that takes only a few minutes but can help improve life for francophones everywhere.

In a nutshell...

The francophone community provides a host of opportunities for the whole family to take part in French-language activities. Whether your youngsters join a sports group, or you enrol in a French course, or your family attends a cultural event, participating in the francophone community can be an enjoyable way to reinforce French in your child's life.

Espace institutionnel

The existence of a French-speaking *espace institutionnel*, or institutional sphere, is an important feature of the francophone education system. It also represents a fundamental difference between francophone and immersion schooling.

In immersion (a program offered by anglophone school boards), French is taught in the classroom as a second language, while English is used elsewhere throughout the system. French-language education, however, is intended for a French-speaking clientele: instruction takes place entirely in French, and at least one parent in the vast majority of section 23 families understands French.

> Just as English is the common language in the anglophone system, French is the common language in the francophone system.

It's only natural, then, that French be used at all levels of the system, from the classroom to the boardroom. In fact, at the school level, French should be the only language heard not only in the classroom, but in the hallways, lunchroom, gymnasium and school grounds. Whenever section 23 parents visit a minority-language school and hear French being used everywhere, they know they've come to the right place.

The institutional sphere includes the classroom, staff room, school administration, school council, parent committees and school board. The consistent use of French in all areas of the institutional sphere reflects the school's *raison d'être*: to serve a francophone clientele.

School councils and school boards

School councils are "collective associations of parents, teachers, secondary students, principals, staff and community representative(s) who work together to effectively support and enhance student learning."[21]

There's no single structure in Canada for the groups of parents who play an advisory role in a school. They're sometimes called parent committees, parent advisory committees, parent action committees, local parent committees or school councils.

They can also include subgroups created for specific purposes, particularly fundraising. Some councils include the principal and staff, others don't. Some have clearly defined powers under the provincial or territorial School Act.

School boards, on the other hand, are the bodies responsible for governing the schools in their jurisdiction. Sometimes they're known as school commissions, school districts, school authorities or regional authorities. Whatever the name, they almost always comprise elected trustees who hire an administration made up of a superintendent, secretary, treasurer and other staff.

Language use by parent groups

One area that's most susceptible to operating in a language other than French is the parent council. As one parent put it, "What difference could it possibly make to our kids if the school council operated in English?"

---

[21] *Alberta School Council Resource Manual.* (Edmonton: Alberta Home and School Councils' Association, 2006), p. II.

On the surface, a council's functioning in English would seem to have no direct impact on the classroom; after all, the two are generally separate parts of the institutional sphere. However, there's a very compelling reason for the school council, like the rest of the system, to function in French: the message it sends children. This is even more significant at the high school level, where one or more student representatives may sit on the school council.

> From an early age, children notice things and reflect on matters more than we think. It's only when they surprise us with a question or comment out of the blue that we sit up and take notice.

Youngsters hear their parents discussing school matters with each other and with other parents. They observe their parents and other adults during school-related activities. They bring home newsletters and other information from the teacher, school administration, parent council and school board. Although they may say nothing, children quickly learn whether French is used only in the classroom or throughout the school system.

> When French is used consistently throughout the system, it sends a clear message to children that communicating *en français* isn't merely an academic exercise confined to the classroom.

Rather, they see French as a relevant language that adults use in the outside world as well. Knowing that adults use French in real-life situations validates students' francophone educational experience. In many respects, this kind of positive reinforcement helps make their schooling an affirmative life experience—which is why francophone rights were established in the first place!

It's a very important message because, outside the minority francophone education system, much of society operates in English, which tends to elevate the status of English in children's minds. If they know that adults use French every day in a larger setting they can relate to, their appreciation of the language will be greater, and their perception of both French and English is more likely to be positive and balanced.

A delicate balance

This is the challenge facing every francophone school, parent council and school board across the country: to strike the delicate balance between preserving a French institutional sphere and enabling non-French-speaking parents to play a meaningful role within it.

It's a complex challenge for many reasons. That's because francophone education is very young and many of the people who are involved in it—after years of being rebuffed by provincial governments and anglophone school boards—are extremely wary of losing what they fought so long and hard to gain.

They're dedicated to promoting a French-speaking institutional sphere not with the goal of excluding anyone, but in order to preserve a system created for all children with francophone roots. Many of these individuals don't even think in terms of *espace institutionnel*—they just know what feels right for them.

Complicating matters is the fact that bilingual francophones often switch into English in the presence of a non-francophone, even when he or she tries to converse in French. For francophones, it's just a matter of courtesy, but for non-francophones, it can be frustrating: they're trying to speak French, but feel like they're being told not to bother.

Although it can be frustrating for both sides, the fact remains that, in a room of a dozen bilingual francophones and one unilingual anglophone, the discussion often takes place in English. So much for a French-speaking *espace institutionnel*!

Another complicating factor is parents and administrators who don't agree that the institutional sphere must retain its French identity. They know that most of their francophone peers are bilingual, and see no reason why everyone on the parent council doesn't just speak English in order to get things done. What they don't realize is that this is the first step in creating an English-language body that will eventually lose its French character altogether.

> Besides sending a contradictory message to children about the nature of the French-language school, an English-language council ignores the very reason minority francophone education exists.

Finally, functioning in English can create significant language and psychological barriers for francophone parents, if for no other reason than it suggests their aspirations—and those of the minority community—are not being respected.

In a nutshell...

The *espace institutionnel* of the French-language school system must reflect the fact that French lies at the very heart of the school's existence. The challenge that school communities across Canada face is to ensure that all parts of the institutional sphere remain French, yet are flexible enough to enable non-French-speaking parents to participate too.

Tips for francophone parents, staff and administrators

⇒ Respect and maintain the French-speaking character of the *espace institutionnel*.

⇒ Address all parents in French. When non-francophone parents make an effort to speak French, encourage them—don't immediately switch into English.

⇒ Respect non-francophone parents' desire to participate in their children's education, and their need to use their mother tongue.

⇒ Remember that all parents, both francophone and non-francophone, have enrolled their children in the francophone system because they want their children to have a meaningful educational and life experience in French. For francophone education to be relevant, it must incorporate language, culture and community.

⇒ Remember too that many non-francophone parents have agreed that their children be educated in French knowing full well that their own participation will be limited because they aren't fluent in the language.

⇒ Make those parents feel welcome at all levels of the francophone educational system, while at the same time maintaining its French character. This means ensuring that French remains the language of communication except when interacting with non-French-speaking parents.

⇒ Encourage all parents to communicate in French, but don't reject those who are unable to do so.

⇒ If you're on the school council and also speak a non-francophone parent's mother tongue, offer to help that person prepare for council meetings by discussing the issues and providing some keywords in French so that he or she can follow and participate in the discussion.

⇒ Remember that your children will value French more if they see that it's respected and relevant in the adult world.

Tips for non-francophone parents

⇒ Understand and respect the fact that every part of the institutional sphere in a French-language school must be French.

⇒ Expect to be greeted in French whenever you visit your children's francophone school. The use of French at the school helps make your children's educational experience relevant. So instead of being upset or offended, join in!

⇒ Make an effort to speak French in and around the school, even if your French isn't that good. If you know only a few words, use them—it's better than not trying at all!

⇒ Think of your children: what message do you send them when you speak nothing but English in their francophone school?

⇒ Remember that francophone parents have fought long and hard for the right to francophone education, and do not want to lose what they have won. Remember too that the battles are far from over.

⇒ Let francophone parents know that you share their desire to create a meaningful French-language educational and life experience for all the children in the school.

⇒ If you understand more French than you speak, insist that your francophone peers communicate in French even though you have to use English to express your ideas.

⇒ Keep up to date on school matters. If this means insisting that your francophone spouse translate school documents for you, so be it! It's hard to play a meaningful role if you don't know what's going on in the school.

⇒ If you wish to participate in school council meetings, familiarize yourself with the issues beforehand and learn some keywords in French so you can better follow and participate in the discussion.

⇒ Remember that your children will value French more if they see that it's respected and relevant in the adult world.

6. Going to school

So you've thought (that's *thought*, not *fought*!) long and hard, and are ready to send your child to a French-language school. Maybe she or he is already attending one, and you're dealing with the reality of being a less-than-fluent parent in a school that's quite unlike the one you attended when you were growing up.

> Some parents choose francophone education knowing they'll face challenges because they don't master French. This truly is a significant and selfless decision—one made for the sole benefit of their children.

For the record, we've had the pleasure of meeting quite a few such parents in different parts of the country, and hold them in the highest esteem.

Focus on French—again

This chapter could be called "Focus on French 2," since it deals with the other major source of French (the other pot o' gold, as it were) that will help your child become fully bilingual: the French-language school. More specifically, we'll look at how you can get involved in your child's schooling.

As we saw in Chapter 4, a framework can be useful for parents who want to help their children develop French as a mother tongue. The francophone school provides another such context that enables children to learn and master French, and to develop the francophone component of their identity.

> The ideal learning framework combines family life and school.

Before we look at ways to bring the two together, though, here's a little story we'd like to share:

A truly sad tale

nce upon a time, a primary francophone school organized a silent auction to raise funds for some much-needed playground equipment. This was a school-wide project: every single child produced a work of art that would be sold the evening of the auction.

Parents were offered the possibility to buy their children's artwork, well in advance, for the modest sum of $5. (The school had a policy whereby no family was prevented from participating in any activity, including this one, for lack of money.) Pre-purchased artwork would still be displayed the evening of the auction, but it would bear a "Sold" sticker.

When the day of the auction finally arrived, the excited students set up rows of tables in the gymnasium (with the help of some parents, not all of whom could speak French) to display their masterpieces. By the end of the day, an impressive array of original artwork awaited the families who would show up that evening!

The auction was a success... though not for everyone. You see, more than a few pieces of art remained on the tables at the end of the evening, most without a "Sold" sticker. The volunteers who helped dismantle the displays were disheartened to think of the children whose parents hadn't bothered to support them and the school initiative, either by purchasing artwork in advance or by coming out to the auction.

When asked about the leftover pieces, one teacher replied, "I'm sad, but not surprised, when I see whose artwork is still here. We teachers know which parents are interested and involved in their kids' education, and which ones aren't, because what happens at home is reflected in students' attitude and performance in the classroom."

This story didn't really happen "once upon a time"; it occurred just a few years ago. Can you imagine what those kids thought their education was worth in their parents' eyes? The teacher's comments show that parents have an impact—whether positive or negative—on their children's schooling.

> One of the most basic things parents can do is take an active interest in their children's education. It sounds too simple, but the effects of encouraging—or not encouraging—children are deep and long-lasting.

Keep this story in mind when you're wondering how to get involved in your child's schooling; it might be easier than you think to have a positive impact!

In your child's shoes

By now, you probably have an idea of what to expect if you enrol your child in a francophone school. For example, you likely know that all the instruction takes place in French except for English Language Arts and other language courses. But what exactly does that mean for your child? Let's try on his or her shoes...

Children attending a francophone school need to master French because that's the language in which they're taught. Their education is also geared not only to academic success but to the development of a francophone identity.

If you were in your child's shoes, how much French would you want to know? To help you answer, we've prepared a little exercise: it's a table for you to fill in, followed by a brief explanation of what the three categories mean.

How much French would you like to know...

... if you were in these grades:	How much French:		
	none	some	lots
• before starting kindergarten			
• after 3 months of kindergarten			
• after 6 months of kindergarten			
• after a year of kindergarten			
• at the start of Grade 1			
• at the end of Grade 1			
• at the start of Grade 2			
• at the end of Grade 2			
• at the start of Grade 3			
• at the end of Grade 3			

What the categories mean

None:
⟹ You cannot understand your teacher or other students.
⟹ You cannot make yourself understood.

Some:
⟹ You can occasionally understand your teacher and classmates.
⟹ You can occasionally make yourself understood by those around you.

(This column could be divided into many degrees: "very little," "a bit more," "more," "more and more," "almost lots," and so on. We'll leave that up to your imagination.)

Lots:
⟹ You can understand everything those around you say.
⟹ You can make yourself understood by everyone around you.

How closely do your answers at the various grades reflect your child's situation today? For example, if your child speaks virtually no French right now and will be starting kindergarten next week, can you reasonably expect her or him to have reached the "some" column after three or six months? (The quick answer is yes; kids in francophone schools start to pick up French impressively fast.)

In light of your family situation, can you map out the progress you think your child can make in the coming three, six and 12 months?

> Regardless of children's French-language skills when they start attending a francophone school, their parents and teachers can always help them improve.

Consider sharing the results of this short exercise with your child's teacher; it's important for her or him to know what you want for your child. Together, you can discuss what each of you can do to help your youngster learn more French and be comfortable at school.

Working together

The most effective way to ensure that children have a positive educational experience is for parents to work as a team with teachers and other staff. This partnership, however, includes a dimension that makes it unique: the French language.

How do you interact with the principal, teachers and support staff at your children's French-language school if you speak little or no French? Some parents hesitate to say so much as "hello" because they don't want to introduce English into the school atmosphere. Others have no qualms about speaking Shakespeare's language (though somewhat updated, of course) with anyone and everyone they meet.

The staff's approach may be equally diverse for various reasons, including their own ability to speak English. This sounds like a recipe for... well, if not disaster, at least confusion!

> One of the easiest things non-francophone parents can do is say *"Bonjour"* whenever they meet someone—staff, other parents, their own and other children—in the school or on the school grounds. It's the most basic gesture that conveys more than a simple greeting.

Even if the rest of your conversation takes place in English, a greeting like *Bonjour* acknowledges that French is important in the school. You might also find that trying out your French with staff members induces some of them to teach you a few more words. What better way to pick up a bit of the language?

By using even a minimum amount of French whenever you're at the school, you show understanding, respect and support for the staff's role in educating your youngsters. You recognize that the teachers' language and cultural identity helps make your children's schooling more relevant.

> Francophone educators throughout Canada are paying more and more attention to the role they play in students' identity development. Besides teaching, these adults serve as role models who have considerable influence on young people.

Now, some non-francophone parents aren't always comfortable trying to speak French in their kids' school. A few will even sprint through the hallways just to avoid having to speak to anyone! It seems that making mistakes in another language bothers some adults more than others.

If it helps at all, we have yet to meet a parent who was laughed at when trying to speak French with staff in a French-language school. On the contrary, francophones appreciate the effort, even if many of them automatically reply in English (that's more a reflex than a criticism of someone's ability to speak French).

If you'd like to overcome any feelings of awkwardness you may have at the idea of speaking French, the best approach is simply to try. In so doing, you'll send a strong message to your child that you value the language that is a key element of his or her identity.

Enrolling your child in a francophone school is a concrete way to show that French is important to you and your spouse. Speaking French in the school, even if you make mistakes, reinforces that message.

Here's what an English teacher who works in a French-language school once said about it:

> *"Before I started teaching here, I didn't speak a word of French and knew nothing about Franco-Canadian culture. Today, I'm part of a community that I didn't even know existed before.*
>
> *There's no reason whatsoever for non-francophone parents not to try speaking French in a francophone school. After all, teachers are experts in "mistake management!" We know how to help without discouraging, which is what allows both children and parents to learn.*

Personally, I love learning French even if the students sometimes find it funny. The first things a non-francophone parent should learn are words that make children smile, and words of encouragement. Anyone can learn to say très bien *and* bravo!"

By the way, whenever you leave the school, don't forget to say "*Au revoir*"!

In a nutshell...

The personnel—that is, the teachers, support staff and administrators—all contribute to the relevance of your child's educational experience. You can reinforce their role, as well as the *raison d'être* of the school, by helping to maintain a French atmosphere in and around the school.

Volunteering in the classroom

Do you want to get involved in the classroom? Start by meeting with your child's teacher and sharing your ideas. In this age of electronic communications, there's still nothing like a face-to-face meeting to forge personal ties.

> Find out how comfortable the teacher feels speaking English, and tell her or him how you feel about speaking French, and English, in the school environment. Once you've discussed these and other questions, seek the common ground that will let you play a role that's both helpful to the teacher and fulfilling for you.

Keep in mind that many variables will influence what you can do. For example, in some classes—especially in early grades—there may be a high percentage of children who speak more English than French. The presence in the classroom of a parent who speaks no French usually incites those youngsters to speak even more English.

If that's the makeup of your child's classroom and you don't speak much French, you might have to redirect your energy elsewhere, such as to the library, at least for a while. Check back regularly with the teacher, though; as the children become more fluent, the classroom dynamic will change from mostly English to mostly French. Teachers often find this happens after the Christmas break.

All volunteer work is valuable!

Some non-French-speaking parents feel they're intentionally being excluded when the teacher asks them to prepare materials, make photocopies and so on, much of which is done outside the classroom. What they want is to help *in* the classroom, despite the fact they don't speak French.

Unfortunately for those parents, it's essential to create and maintain a French-speaking atmosphere in order to provide students with a meaningful francophone education. There's just no way of getting around this reality.

In any case, the importance of preparing materials shouldn't be underestimated! It's a time-consuming job. By performing such tasks, parents can enable teachers to concentrate on helping students—which is what they're trained to do.

Presentations

Sometimes parents are invited to speak to their children's class about their profession or other areas of expertise. If you're interested in giving a presentation, don't just assume that all the students understand English.

Meet with the teacher well in advance to draw up a list of keywords in French. Then use them: practise saying them beforehand; refer to the list during your presentation (even if most of your presentation is in English); write the words on the blackboard or distribute copies.

Use as much French as you can—and, above all, don't fret over your language skills! Kids are much more accepting than we give them credit for.

Inviting non-francophone parents to give presentations to their children's class is a positive, realistic gesture. It recognizes the fact that many children in francophone schools come from mixed households.

What can be a problem, though, is a parent's deciding to give a presentation entirely in English simply because he or she isn't a francophone.

Needless to say, there is a better way! Anyone can follow the above suggestions to make a presentation relevant to a French-speaking audience—which is exactly what those students are.

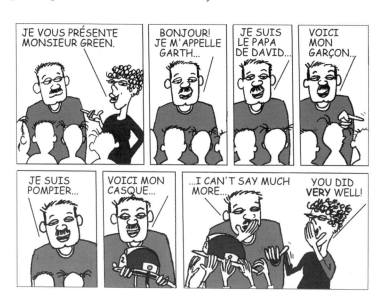

In a nutshell...

Volunteers are a valuable asset in any school, and every bit of help they give is important. A parent's role in the classroom depends on many variables that must be discussed beforehand with the teacher. When you think of how you'd like to help, remember that it's essential to maintain a French-speaking atmosphere in your child's classroom. Remember, too, that there's no such thing as a meaningless task!

Tips for parents

⇒ If you want to volunteer in the classroom, meet with your child's teacher to identify your respective comfort levels, and then find the common ground that will satisfy you both.

⇒ Be aware of the fact that many teachers accept only limited use of English in their classroom because they want and need to maintain a strong French-speaking atmosphere.

⇒ No matter what task you end up doing, remember that every bit of assistance helps enhance the educational experience for all children.

⇒ If you're going to give a presentation in the classroom, meet with the teacher in advance to draw up a list of keywords in French. Use the list during your presentation; write the words on the blackboard or distribute copies.

In parents' own words...

As we mentioned earlier in this chapter, we've met a lot of mixed Canadian couples who have children in francophone schools. Many of them have found satisfying ways to participate actively in their kids' education. Here are some ideas that come up frequently, along with a few parents' comments:

Attend all school functions.

⇒ *"We attend all the functions we can. It helps our children feel welcome as well. They like to show what they're learning and they like that we participate and support them."*

⇒ *"Even if I don't understand what people are saying all the time, I enjoy watching my own and other people's kids and want them to know I support them 100 percent."*

⇒ *"It's important for me to show my daughter that what she's doing in her francophone school is important, that she's learning her father's language and I'm very proud of that."*

⇒ *"I've helped out for the past two years at our school's open house because there are often English-French couples dropping by and they're glad to have the point of view of an English-speaking parent who's been around for a while. It's something I can do where my language isn't an obstacle, it's an advantage!"*

⇒ *"I always attend the school concerts, plays etc. and I always bring my parents who don't speak a word of French. I want our boys to know that their English-speaking dad and grandparents are really proud of them."*

⇒ *"It's not in the school, but I help out by 'recruiting' new students whenever I hear families speaking French at the grocery store or in the mall. I just introduce myself, ask if their children are in school and where, and tell them about our excellent francophone school. Most of them didn't even know there was a school like that in town! They thought their only choice was immersion."*

Attend parent-teacher interviews.

⇒ *"My husband is the francophone in the family. This year, the parent-teacher interviews always take place in French because the teacher has just moved out from Quebec and doesn't speak much English at all. So my husband and I discuss things ahead of time, make a list of questions we want to ask, take the sheet along, and he jots down the main things the teacher says. I find that I'm actually able to follow along more than I thought I could, since she shows us our son's work so I have a point of reference. After the interview, my husband and I sit down and he fills me in on whatever I didn't catch. It's important for me to show the teacher that I'm interested even though she and I can't communicate very easily together. So far our system is working well."*

⇒ *"We hold the first part of the interview in French with our daughter present, then she goes off with her mother while I discuss things with the teacher in English."*

⇒ *"I always attend the parent-teacher interviews and support the teacher by being involved in my son's education. I enquire about his progress, and work with him at home on skills that do not require French."*

Volunteer in the classroom.

⇒ *"At the beginning of the year, the teacher told us that she welcomed help from parents who didn't speak French but wanted to make sure French was the language of the classroom. So that was very clear from the outset. She also told us there weren't enough aides in the school and she spent a lot of time preparing. So that's mostly what I do, preparing things, although my French is improving and now I'm able to help some of the children with their math problems too."*

⇒ *"I met with the English teacher and told him I wanted to volunteer. Every week, I spend a morning reading stories to different groups, while the teacher works with other students who need more attention."*

⇒ *"I can't go to my kids' school during the day, but one thing I do is tell them they have to speak French in the classroom, in the halls, in the playground, everywhere. That's not really volunteering, I suppose, but I know it helps the teacher anyway. And otherwise my kids are missing the whole point of being in that school in the first place."*

Help out elsewhere in the school.

⇒ *"I help out in the library. When our school first started up, I helped clean and repair books that we inherited from somewhere, and I put on bar codes for their computerized system. If that sounds boring, well, it was. But there were a few of us who worked on the project, and we'd go for coffee afterwards and have become good friends. I still help out in the library because I love books and there's always something to do—and it's much more interesting now that all the basic things have been taken care of. I'm also learning quite a bit of French!"*

⇒ *"We hold a special lunch once a month, and I help organize and run it. You don't need to speak French in order to count money, and I've learned the French words I need when I help serve. 'Un morceau ou deux? Plus de lait?' It's not hard!"*

⇒ *"I am very self-conscious about speaking so little French, so I participate in activities where language is not a barrier. I help set up tables and chairs, put up decorations, clean up after events. These are the same kinds of things I would do if my children were in an English school."*

Accompany classes on outings.

⇒ *"Many outings don't require a lot of language use except to keep a group of children in order and take care of the usual kid things. I feel that my presence just reflects the reality of our family—a francophone parent and an anglophone parent. Being with my son's class for a day or even half-day outing gives me a chance to get to know his classmates, and I'm also helping the teacher."*

⇒ *"My company gives employees one 'school day' off every three months just to do something at our children's school. I schedule those days for when there's an outing because my French isn't good enough for the classroom, and outings are special days that I like to be a part of. My son is proud to have me there and to show me how well he can speak French."*

Participate in school decisions and on committees.

⇒ *"Our parent council sometimes has committees that operate in English because they deal almost exclusively with matters that require the use of English. A year ago I was on a playground committee, where everything we did involved dealing with local businesses and the City, all of it in English. There were four of us, and we performed an important service for the school. We worked on that project for months, giving our reports in English at the school council meetings even though the rest of the meetings were in French. The whole council really appreciated our work. They also thanked us personally in their newsletter, which was great because it allowed all the francophone parents in the school to see that anglos were part of the team."*

⇒ *"From the day we first enrolled our child, I have made a point of keeping up on all the school policies and practices. In fact, I looked into the school policies before we even decided to send our child here. I make appointments to meet with the principal and give him my feedback on matters of concern to me. The fact that I don't speak much French does not mean I can't influence policies that affect my child, and the principal seems to appreciate my input."*

⇒ *"I take part in parent meetings without worrying about what others might say. I understand way more French than I speak, but that doesn't stop me from saying everything I want in passable Franglais! I insist that the other parents continue to speak French, and they can correct me if they want as long as it's not too often. As long as we understand each other in French, that's all that matters."*

Support your francophone spouse's involvement.

⇒ *"I stay home with the kids so that my spouse can attend evening meetings and some weekend conventions. Needless to say, she's very involved in the francophone community. I can also work at home sometimes, which allows her to carry out official business during the day."*

⇒ *"I make my husband go to all the parent council meetings, which he actually enjoys but wouldn't make time for if I didn't insist. Last week he came home and said he'd gotten himself onto a fund-raising committee, and he was full of ideas and enthusiasm. Guess I won't have to insist so much next month!"*

In a nutshell...

Non-francophone parents have many opportunities to get involved at the school level. Attending school functions, going to parent-teacher interviews, volunteering in the classroom, helping out elsewhere in the school, joining in class outings, participating in school decisions and on committees, actively supporting your francophone spouse's involvement—these are just a few of the possibilities. It all depends on your personality, schedule and comfort in French. No matter what activity you choose, you're showing your children that their education is important to you. If your work or home situation prevents you from helping out during the day at the school, you can still do a lot at home. There are many, many ways you can help your child have a positive educational experience!

Homework

When asked about the challenges of having their children attend a francophone school, many non-French-speaking parents immediately answer "homework."

> There's no denying that French-speaking spouses are generally better able to help with homework. This is something both parents should realize before enrolling their children in a francophone school.

And yet... and yet... non-francophone spouses can help much more than many of them realize.

The old standbys

First, let's trot out the old standbys: Math and English. Take a few minutes to learn how to say numbers and some mathematical operations in French, and you'll be able to help your kids for a few years without having to return to school yourself. After a while, though, you might have some difficulty—as will more than a few francophone parents, since the teaching of math is constantly evolving.

As for English, if it's your mother tongue, it's probably one of your children's mother tongues, too. You have enough material right there to be happily busy helping them for as long as they're in school.

There, we've covered the two subjects that come up whenever non-francophone parents ask how they can get involved in their children's homework. But make no mistake: with effort and dedication on your part, those two subjects can keep you busy for a long time.

Now for a deeper look at this question...

Take time

You want to do more, but how much time are you willing or able to invest in helping your child with his or her homework? Even parents who face no language barrier can find it difficult to be as involved as they'd like. That's because...

> It takes time and commitment to help kids with their homework!

It can mean putting aside your own projects and sitting down with your child for anything from minutes to hours. It can mean missing certain TV shows, or not listening to the radio as you prepare supper, or not talking on the phone with your friends. It can mean putting off some things—and then doing them later, after your youngster is sound asleep.

Oh yes, then there's that minor detail of your French-language abilities.

⇒ It can be frustrating not to be able to understand all the assignments that your child brings home from school. That's where your partnership with the teacher comes in handy: let her or him know your situation (your francophone spouse may not be around to read and translate for you), and together you'll no doubt find a solution. Some schools have a buddy system to help in situations like that.

⇒ It's also difficult to help when you can't understand what your youngster has written. Once again, if you're in a situation where you don't have your spouse's help, let the teacher know.

Start early...

It's easiest to help your child with homework when he or she is young. For example, if there are words to study for dictations, you can help by reading them aloud so your child can write them down. Don't worry about your accent or pronunciation! Kids are clever enough that they'll know what you're saying—

most of the time, at least. And when they don't, well, they'll be able to figure things out with a bit of help from you.

Once you've finished dictating the words, you can go over your child's work by comparing her or his spelling with that of the word list. You don't have to be fluent in French to be able to do that!

> By starting early, you and your child can develop work habits where it's natural for you to help regardless of your accent or limited French-language skills.

Some couples function as a team, each helping with certain subjects or at certain times, with the francophone spouse providing translation when necessary.

... and continue for a long, long time

If your circumstances are such that you feel you can't help your child with homework because you don't know enough French, there are still things you can do. Here's an approach some parents have used with great success once their children are old enough to read:

⇒ Ask your child to translate the assignment into your mother tongue so you know what the teacher wants.

⇒ When you've understood the assignment, send your child off to do the work.

⇒ Once the work is finished, ask your child to translate it orally into your mother tongue so you can assess his or her work.

Some people think translation is simple. Not so! It's a very complex activity that requires highly nuanced understanding and an ability to express oneself clearly. There's a good reason why researchers in the field of artificial intelligence use translation as a way to test their latest devices.

When students translate their homework for their parents, they must have grasped the concepts or their translation won't make sense.

> This is a time-consuming but highly effective way to help children with their homework.

In addition to ensuring they do their homework correctly, you show that you're interested in all their schoolwork. It's a powerful message, and absolutely vital to their schooling. One of the key findings of a recent international study is that, across social and economic lines, the more interest parents show in their children's education, the more their children will get out of their schooling.[1]

Some schools have set up after-hours homework clubs where students do their homework under supervision. Depending on your family circumstances, this could be a valid option for your children. If your school doesn't have such a club, suggest to the principal or school council that one be set up (bearing in mind that transportation could be an issue).

---

[1] PISA 2000.

Older students can always help their younger sisters and brothers, especially if their efforts are recognized in some meaningful way. If there are no older siblings in your family, perhaps your friends (or "buddies" if your school has a buddy system) have older French-speaking children who would like to help.

Lastly, you can always send out an SOS! More specifically, you can turn to *SOS Devoirs* ("SOS Homework"), a French-language tutoring service available to students from grades 1 to 12 in many francophone schools across the country. Here's the link: **www.sosdevoirs.org**.

In a nutshell...

There are many ways you can help your child with homework. When he or she is younger, it's not too difficult to read French dictation words or help with math. Later, you can get him or her to translate assignments so you can understand. The key is to show you're interested in your child's education by dedicating time to helping with homework. It's also important that your child's teacher be aware of your family situation if your francophone spouse isn't there to help.

7. The Francophonie

The international Francophonie

You may have heard of the international Francophonie, but do you know exactly what it is? The term first appeared in France in 1880 to describe French-speaking peoples and countries around the world. The Francophonie movement began in earnest in the 1960s as former French colonies sought to redefine their relationship with France. Throughout the decade, international francophone associations were founded in various fields, including education, sports, law and politics.

In 1970, a permanent body was formed to promote multilateral government cooperation. The first Francophonie Summit was held in Paris in 1986, and in 1997 the first Secretary-General of the Organisation Internationale de la Francophonie (OIF) was elected: Boutros Boutros-Ghali accepted the position after having served a term as Secretary-General of the United Nations.

Today, the OIF encompasses 55 member states that are home to some 200 million French-speaking people. The Francophonie covers a considerable portion of the world's population; in many respects, it's similar to the Commonwealth, which brings together member states of the former British Empire. Canada is one of the few countries to belong to both.

A look at Canada

According to the 2001 Census, over 6.7 million Canadians have French as a mother tongue, some 940,000 of whom live outside Quebec. The latter group has been steadily declining for decades now. Many francophones aren't passing on the language to their children, and one of the reasons is that they're not speaking French at home.

In 2001, of the 940,000 people outside Quebec whose mother tongue is French, less than 62 percent spoke French most often at home. Thirty years earlier, the figure was 73 percent.

It's not surprising, then, that the proportion of individuals outside Quebec with French as a mother tongue dropped from 5.95 percent in 1971 to 4.4 percent in 2001.

Here are a few other statistics you might find interesting: in 2001, the rate of exogamy among the general francophone population outside Quebec was 42 percent. However, among francophone section 23 rights holders (in other words, parents of children under 18), the national figure was closer to 60 percent.

> To put it another way, almost twice as many francophone parents across Canada are now living in mixed relationships as are living with another francophone.

Those are just a few of the many statistics we could cite when describing the Francophonie within Canada. And while it's often true that statistics can be used to prove any point, the figures speak volumes about how that nation-wide community is evolving. At least the numbers are relevant, unlike...

The irrelevant numbers game

Many section 23 parents have had the following question put to them at one time or another: "Why should francophones have the right to publicly funded schools and school boards when there are more Canadians who speak Chinese (or Italian, or German, or Polish, or Spanish, or Portuguese, etc.)?"

The answer: it has nothing to do with numbers!

Rather, it's a constitutional right enshrined in the Canadian Charter of Rights and Freedoms. This is the highest law in the land, and as such it helps define Canada as a bilingual and multicultural country. The funding of minority-language education, whether French outside Quebec or English inside Quebec, is crucial to maintaining the health of our official languages. People who question this are missing the point that promoting our national identity requires more than paying lip service.

As one non-francophone section 23 parent put it, "I won't apologize to anyone for exercising my constitutional right to enrol my child in a francophone school." Nor should any parent.

Oh, and by the way...

Whoever asks you that question has got it all wrong, anyway: far more Canadians have French as a mother tongue than any other language besides English. And that's even without factoring in the nearly six million francophone Quebeckers!

The impact of exogamy

Having children is a personal choice made by couples, who in the process create a family structure that reflects their individual backgrounds. But when those couples are mixed, and when enough of them decide to have children, exogamy becomes a social phenomenon as well.

The influence of exogamy on Canada's minority francophone population isn't the sort of thing people sit down to read about on a dark and stormy night... hmm... as the rain falls in torrents, except when it's checked by a gust of wind that sweeps up the exogamy-filled streets, rattling along the housetops, and fiercely agitating the scanty flame of the exogamic lamps that struggle heroically against the exogamy-engulfing darkness...

Editor's note: Please excuse the author's totally irrelevant digression. His ghostly (or should that be "ghastly"?) muse is Edward George Bulwer-Lytton, who is credited (by those who credit such things) with having written the worst opening line of any English-language novel. Apparently the author simply could not resist the temptation to add his peculiar twist to this famous passage. Sad, oh so sad.

People's perception is shaped by what they see around them—and what Acadians and francophones around the country often see is children of mixed couples who barely understand French and speak it even less.

The rate of exogamy is steadily rising across Canada, as is the number of children who are losing touch with the French side of their family heritage.

It's no coincidence that the social phenomenon of exogamy is often equated with assimilation, or the erosion of French language and culture outside Quebec.

Associating exogamy with assimilation isn't new, either: scholars as far back as the 1700s were making the connection in their writings on life in the New World.

Although we all use the term *assimilation*, there seems to be no consensus among researchers on exactly what it entails. Some consider it a matter of numbers, whereas others see it as a social phenomenon—much like exogamy.

> The choices you and your spouse make will shape your family structure, which will in turn have an impact on the francophone community and, ultimately, on Canadian society.

For instance, if you and all the other mixed couples around you decided to speak only English to your children and send them to an English school, French language and culture might eventually disappear from your region (depending on the proportion of exogamous couples).

The larger picture

Fortunately, that's not a likely scenario. And on a family level as opposed to a statistical level, exogamy doesn't necessarily mean the erosion of French language and culture whatsoever. If neither language in your household dominates the other, there's no reason for one to suffer from neglect and slowly disappear. As we saw in Chapter 4, the key lies in ensuring that your child is exposed to enough French that he or she will develop it as a mother tongue.

For some mixed couples, that's the ideal situation: creating the conditions for children to become fluently bilingual and fully develop their dual heritage. But statistics show that many other couples don't make this choice:

> Nationally, fewer than half the children of section 23 rights holders have French as a mother tongue. That number drops to less than a quarter in exogamous households.[23]

It's a different story for families with two francophone parents: over 90 percent of their children have French as a mother tongue, although in some parts of the country the figure is considerably lower.

Statistics also show that the higher the percentage of mixed couples, the lower the proportion of children who learn French at home and receive a francophone education. Whether or not the situation changes in the coming years—given that francophone schools haven't been around very long yet—remains to be seen.

There are always exceptions individually, locally, regionally and provincially, and various factors can affect the statistics: government policies, the level of bilingualism among non-francophone parents, the strength of francophone communities, and so on. But the fact remains that the children of many mixed

---

[23] Rodrigue Landry, *Libérer le potentiel caché de l'exogamie*. (Commission nationale des parents francophones, 2003).

couples, and those of quite a few francophone couples, aren't learning French as a mother tongue.

One of the main impacts on the francophone education system is a potential student population that far exceeds the actual number of children attending francophone schools. There are many section 23 parents out there, but where are they? And why are their children receiving an education that will probably lead to their losing French as a mother tongue?

In a nutshell...

Exogamy as a social phenomenon is strongly linked to assimilation. Statistics show an inverse relationship between exogamy and both the learning of French at home and enrolment in French-language schools. However, there is no reason that the children of mixed couples cannot develop the francophone component of their identity.

The Canadian Francophonie

In the following pages, we'll visit—in alphabetical order—each of the provinces and territories across Canada except for Quebec (our focus being on Canada's minority, not majority, French-speaking population). Here's what you'll find:

⇒ The francophone flag of the province or territory. Unfortunately, it'll be in black, white and shades of grey, but at least you'll get a general idea of its makeup. If you want to see these flags in all their glorious colour, you'll find them on our website: **www.exogam.ca**.

⇒ A brief general history of the province or territory, especially the role played by francophones or Acadians.

⇒ An equally brief look at French-language education. In some cases, you'll read about how francophones and Acadians were deprived of the possibility to have their children educated in their mother tongue, and for how long that situation lasted. Translate those years into generations, then imagine all the francophone children who were educated exclusively in English, and you'll see how easily a language can disappear from a family tree.

⇒ Statistics, or "Stats at a glance." Now, a word is in order: we pored over statistics, statistics and more statistics until everything turned blurry, including our ability to think. We could show you a dozen figures representing the same statistic (such as "rate of exogamy"), all based on raw data from the 2001 Census, and no two will be the same. It's maddeningly difficult to find consistency—in fact, we're starting to suspect that presenting statistical data is similar to forecasting the weather!

Anyway, we've chosen a few figures we consider relevant and reliable, including a breakdown of people who have French as a mother tongue.

Also included is the proportion of mixed couples among section 23 rights holders in each province and territory, according to the national federation of French-language school boards. We've seen different (sometimes significantly different) figures on this topic elsewhere, so you might want to consider these, and the other numbers, to be a general indicator.

One last word about the stats: these are all based on the 2001 Census; language-related data from the 2006 Census will start becoming available on the Statistics Canada website, **www.statscan.ca**, on December 4, 2007. We'll also feature a few interesting and relevant figures at **www.exogam.ca**.

Alberta

A very brief history[24,25]

In the early 1700s, French and other European explorers ventured across the prairies toward the Rockies. *Coureurs des bois*, the North-West Mounted Police and settlers soon followed. A French-Canadian NWMP officer established Fort Calgary, while French was the dominant language in the early days of Fort Edmonton. Arriving in the mid-1800s, French-speaking priests set out to colonize their parishes by recruiting francophones from the east. Another wave of French-speaking migrants in the late 19th century and the first half of the 20th century led to the founding of numerous villages in the northeast and northwest of the province. The westward migration continues today, though mostly to the urban centres.

Education[26,27]

The first French-language school in Alberta, when the region was still called the Northwest Territories, was founded in 1842. The Territories were officially bilingual at the time, so citizens had the right to have their children schooled entirely in French. That right remained in effect for only 50 years: in 1892, English became the official language of instruction, and teaching in French was restricted to a single course at the primary level. Not until 1976—fully 84 years later—were Franco-Albertans once again able to have their children educated entirely in French. In 1988, section 23 parents' right to francophone schooling was recognized and, in 1993, francophone governance took effect. As of 2007, five francophone school boards were operating 28 public and Catholic schools around Alberta. French-language schools will continue to open in response to the influx of francophones and Acadians from other parts of Canada.

24 *The Oxford Companion to Canadian History*. (Don Mills: Oxford University Press, 2004).

25 *Franco.ca*. (Ottawa: Fondation ConceptArt multimédia, 2005).

26 Conseil scolaire Centre Nord, 2006.

27 *Annuaire de l'éducation en français au Canada*. (Ottawa: Fédération nationale des conseils scolaires francophones, 2006), pp. 50–54.

Stats at a glance[28]

Total population 2,941,150
French mother tongue 65,990
English mother tongue 2,412,190
Other mother tongues 497,205

Residents who have French as a mother tongue

> *French only* *58,645*
> *French and English* *5,780*
> *French and non-official language* *1,090*
> *French, English and non-official language* *475*

⇒ Francophones account for 2.2 percent of Alberta's population.

⇒ Some 22,000 people speak French most often at home; another 27,000 speak the language regularly, including 11,000 anglophones.

⇒ According to the 2001 Census, over 200,000 Albertans have some knowledge of both official languages.

> There are over 27,000 section 23 rights holders in the province, 75 percent of whom live in exogamous relationships.[29]

The number of Albertans whose mother tongue is French increased by over 12 percent from 1996 to 2001, and the proportion of the population with French as a mother tongue is slightly rising.

Many Franco-Albertans reside in and around Calgary and Edmonton because of the diverse employment opportunities and services. Other francophone communities are located in the northwest region around Peace River and Grande Prairie, and in the northeast around Saint Paul. Quite a few Acadians can be found working in the oil sands near Fort McMurray.

---

[28] *2001 Census.* (Government of Canada, 2002).

[29] *Les ayants droit au Canada.* (Fédération nationale des conseils scolaires francophones, 2003), p. 6.

British Columbia

A very brief history [30,31]

French-Canadian voyageurs were involved in the earliest exploration across the Rocky Mountains, including expeditions by Alexander Mackenzie in 1793 and Simon Fraser several years later. As early as 1807, the voyageurs were building forts and starting to colonize the area. But an influx of English-speaking immigrants in the second half of the 19th century meant that francophones were soon a minority. In 1909, French-speaking migrants from Quebec and from Willow Bunch, Saskatchewan, moved to Maillardville, where they opened a school and founded the first French-language parish in the province. Francophones continue to migrate to British Columbia today, but aren't concentrated in any particular region.

Education [32,33]

Although they had their own schools before BC became a province, francophones have had to fight for their educational rights for much of the last 130 years. In 1967, the premier even declared there would never be a public francophone school in the province. But francophones' tenacity paid off with the opening of the first autonomous public French-language school in 1983. Legal pressure was needed, from 1988 to 1994, to finally bring about the creation of a school board in 1995. The board initially covered only the Lower Mainland and southern Vancouver Island but, following further legal action in 1997, was given jurisdiction over the whole province in 1999. As of 2007, the board was providing a French-language education to over 3,800 students in 38 schools around the province, 20 of which were autonomous.

---

[30] *The Oxford Companion to Canadian History.*

[31] *Franco.ca*, 2005.

[32] Conseil scolaire francophone de la Colombie-Britannique, 2007.

[33] *Annuaire de l'éducation en français au Canada*, pp. 62–66.

Stats at a glance[34]

Total population 3,868,875
French mother tongue 63,630
English mother tongue 2,865,300
Other mother tongues 939,945

Residents who have French as a mother tongue

> *French only* *54,400*
> *French and English* *6,780*
> *French and non-official language* *1,705*
> *French, English and non-official language* *745*

⇒ Francophones account for 1.6 percent of British Columbia's population.

⇒ Some 18,000 people speak French most often at home; another 28,000 speak the language regularly, including 13,000 anglophones and 700 people whose mother tongue is neither French nor English.

⇒ According to the 2001 Census, about 270,000 British Columbians have some knowledge of both official languages.

> There are almost 21,000 section 23 rights holders in the province, 77 percent of whom live in exogamous relationships.[35]

Although the French-speaking population has grown by 50 percent in recent decades, the proportion of francophones has declined slightly. Francophones are present throughout the province. Over 29,000 francophones live in greater Vancouver, a mere 1.5 percent of the metropolis's population, while some 6,000 reside in Victoria, 1.9 percent of the capital's population. Whistler is home to the greatest concentration of francophones, at 5.5 percent of the area's population. Nowhere else in the province do francophones account for a major percentage of the population.

---

[34] *2001 Census.*

[35] *Les ayants droit au Canada*, p. 6.

Manitoba

A very brief history[36,37]

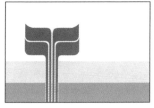

Manitoba, inhabited for centuries by the Cree, Dakota, Dene, Inuit and Ojibwa peoples, was home to scores of francophones well before it became a province in 1870. The first Europeans to venture onto the prairies were French, and the first permanent settlement was founded in 1738 by La Vérendrye at what would later become Saint Boniface. Mixed marriages between French and First Nations inhabitants created a strong, vibrant Métis population that far outnumbered other groups when Manitoba gained provincial status. But French-language development was cut short in 1890 when the legislature declared English to be the only official language (a law that was declared illegal some 80 years later), and in 1916 French schooling was banned. French didn't regain the equivalent place in the education system until more than six decades later.

Education[38,39]

Formal French-language education was first provided in Manitoba when the Grey Nuns reached Saint Boniface in 1844. During the 1900s, however, three generations of francophones were unable to have their children educated in their mother tongue. A 1993 Supreme Court ruling upheld Franco-Manitobans' right to govern their own schools, and the *Division scolaire franco-manitobaine* (DSFM) was created a year later. The DSFM administers French-language education throughout the province, serving both rural and urban centres. Like many of their counterparts across the country, Franco-Manitobans are building or rebuilding their communities around the local school. In 2007, the DSFM was providing a French-language education to students in 23 schools around the province.

---

[36] *The Oxford Companion to Canadian History.*

[37] *Franco.ca*, 2005.

[38] Division scolaire franco-manitobaine, 2007.

[39] *Annuaire de l'éducation en français au Canada*, pp. 80–83.

Stats at a glance[40]

Total population	1,103,695
French mother tongue	47,560
English mother tongue	839,765
Other mother tongues	232,775

Residents who have French as a mother tongue

› French only	44,340
› French and English	2,675
› French and non-official language	435
› French, English and non-official language	110

⇒ Francophones account for 4.3 percent of the province's population. This figure represents a decline from seven percent over the past 50 years. Almost 10 percent of Franco-Manitobans are First Nations citizens, including some 3,000 Métis.

⇒ Some 22,000 people speak French most often at home; another 16,000 speak the language regularly, including 6,000 anglophones.

⇒ According to the 2001 Census, almost 103,000 Manitobans have some knowledge of both official languages.

> There are nearly 18,000 section 23 rights holders in the province, 66 percent of whom live in exogamous relationships.[41]

Today's Franco-Manitobans are mainly urban dwellers, with two-thirds of them living in the Winnipeg area. Over half of those residents live in the former francophone settlements of Saint-Boniface, Saint-Vital, and Saint-Nobert. Likewise, in rural areas, most francophones live in villages and parishes founded by French-speaking settlers.

The Franco-Manitoban population is relatively old: the median age is 46, compared with a provincial average of 36.

---

[40] *2001 Census.*

[41] *Les ayants droit au Canada,* p. 6.

New Brunswick

A very brief history[42,43]

Acadians have lived in New Brunswick since the early 1600s, forming tightly knit communities and developing a unique culture. Their numbers grew slowly over the first century, and then more quickly in 1755 when many of their counterparts from Nova Scotia sought refuge from the deportation. These fine farming folk were forced to move into more remote areas with poor soil, and had to supplement their livelihood with fishing and logging. Although the isolation was an economic handicap, it also allowed the Acadians to develop a vibrant culture complete with French-language schools and hospitals. In more recent times, New Brunswick became Canada's only officially bilingual province in 1969, and the equality of French and English was recognized in 1981. This equality was enshrined in the Canadian Constitution in 1993.

Education[44,45]

Acadians in New Brunswick have had access to French-language schooling, in one form or another, for hundreds of years. In 1871, the government made all public schools non-denominational—a controversial move at the time, but one that ultimately had no long-term adverse effect. In 1974, the Department of Education was reorganized into French and English sectors, and four years later the first minority French-language school-community centre opened in Fredericton. Acadian and francophone parents formed a provincial association in 1988 and later changed the name to *Association francophone des parents du Nouveau-Brunswick*.

As of 2007, five francophone school districts were providing French-language education to some 35,000 students in a hundred schools around the province.

---

[42] *The Oxford Companion to Canadian History.*

[43] *Franco.ca*, 2005.

[44] New Brunswick Department of Education, 2007.

[45] *Annuaire de l'éducation en français au Canada*, pp. 92–104.

Stats at a glance[46]

Total population 720,000
French mother tongue 243,690
English mother tongue 471,010
Other mother tongues 12,625

Residents who have French as a mother tongue

> *French only 236,665*
> *French and English 5,255*
> *French and non-official language 105*
> *French, English and non-official language 35*

⇒ Francophones and Acadians account for 33.2 percent of the province's population.

⇒ In New Brunswick, 220,000 people speak French most often at home, and another 25,000 speak the language regularly.

⇒ According to the 2001 Census, almost 250,000 New Brunswickers have some knowledge of both official languages.

> There are almost 57,000 section 23 rights holders in the province, 25 percent of whom live in exogamous relationships.[47]

New Brunswick's population comprises two main language groups: two-thirds of the population have English as their mother tongue, while almost all the others are French-speaking.

New Brunswick is a fairly rural province, and many inhabitants reside in small rural communities in which francophones form a strong majority. Acadians live mostly along the coast, concentrated in three areas: the Madawaska, the Acadian Peninsula and the southeast part of the province. A few urban centres are also home to major francophone communities, including Edmundston, Bathurst and Moncton/Dieppe.

---

[46] *2001 Census.*

[47] *Les ayants droit au Canada*, p. 6.

Newfoundland and Labrador

A very brief history[48,49]

Prehistoric human presence in the province dates back at least 7,500 years, and was followed by the Innu and Inuit in Labrador and the Beothuk in Newfoundland. Norse explorers arrived in the 10th or 11th century; from the end of the 15th century, fishers from France, England, Spain and Portugal plied the waters around the island. The French founded a settlement in Plaisance (Placentia) in the 1660s, which incited the British to establish their own permanent presence on the island. Although the French accepted British sovereignty some 50 years later, they successfully settled what became known as the French Shore over the next century. The French-speaking population increased in the mid-1800s when Acadian farmers settled in the Bay St. George area. Today, fishing and farming have been replaced by employment in public administration, education, business and construction.

Education[50,51]

The first French-language school in Newfoundland and Labrador opened its doors in La Grand'Terre in 1984. Five years later, the provincial francophone parents federation was created in order to lobby for better educational services. Their lobbying, aided by the Supreme Court's Mahé decision, led to the 1997 creation of a French-language school board to govern francophone education throughout the province. As of 2007, the board was operating five schools, located in Cap Saint-Georges, Goose Bay, La Grand'Terre, Labrador City and Saint John's. The establishments in La Grand'Terre and Saint John's are school-community centres.

48 *The Oxford Companion to Canadian History.*

49 *Franco.ca,* 2007.

50 Conseil scolaire francophone provincial de Terre-Neuve et Labrador, 2007.

51 *Annuaire de l'éducation en français au Canada,* pp. 180–181.

Stats at a glance[52]

Total population 547,140
French mother tongue 2,450
English mother tongue 539,048
Other mother tongues 5,663

Residents who have French as a mother tongue
> *French only* *2,110*
> *French and English* *330*
> *French and non-official language* *0*
> *French, English and non-official language* *10*

⇒ Francophones account for 0.5 percent of the province's population.

⇒ Some 1,000 people speak French most often at home; another 2,000 speak the language regularly, including 400 anglophones.

⇒ According to the 2001 Census, almost 21,000 residents of Newfoundland and Labrador have some knowledge of both official languages.

> There are 985 section 23 rights holders in the province, 68 percent of whom live in exogamous relationships.[53]

The number of francophones in Newfoundland and Labrador has steadily declined over the last decade. Francophones are concentrated mainly in three areas: the Port-au-Port Peninsula, St. John's and Labrador. There are some 700 francophones in each of these regions, and they account for over 15 percent of the population in the Cap-Saint-Georges area of the Port-au-Port Peninsula. Of the 655 francophones living on the Avalon Peninsula (including St. John's), many are from other Atlantic provinces, Quebec, and the French island of Saint-Pierre.

---

[52] *2001 Census.*

[53] *Les ayants droit au Canada*, p. 6.

Northwest Territories

A very brief history[54],[55]

The Northwest Territories once constituted the largest region of Canada. The area was bought from the Hudson's Bay Company in 1870, and had major sections carved off to form Manitoba in 1870, the Yukon in 1898, and Saskatchewan and Alberta in 1905. Ontario and Quebec were enlarged from the Territories in 1912; the remaining land was further divided in 1999 to create Nunavut. Francophones were among the first non-natives to visit the present-day NWT, including a French-Canadian who founded Fort Resolution in 1786. From the earliest days of colonization and well into the 1800s, francophones made up half the population. They helped form settlements around trading posts and Catholic missions, forging strong links with First Nations residents. At the turn of the century, however, government policies made English the only official language and the language of education. Francophones had to wait until 1984 for a new Official Languages act, which wasn't fully implemented until 1993.

Education[56],[57]

Section 23 rights holders began lobbying the NWT government in the early 1980s for a French-language school; their efforts paid off in 1989 with the founding of École Alain St-Cyr in Yellowknife. In 1995, the government adopted a bill recognizing francophones' right to govern their schools, and in 2000 the *Commission scolaire francophone de division* was created. A second French-language school, in Hay River, opened its doors the following year. École Alain St-Cyr underwent an expansion in 2006 that was expected to be completed by September 2007.

---

[54] *The Oxford Companion to Canadian History.*

[55] *Franco.ca*, 2006.

[56] Association des parents ayants droit de Yellowknife, 2007.

[57] *Annuaire de l'éducation en français au Canada*, pp. 184–186.

Stats at a glance[58]

Total population 37,105
French mother tongue 1,060
English mother tongue 29,080
Other mother tongues 7,425

Residents who have French as a mother tongue
> French only 950
> French and English 85
> French and non-official language 15
> French, English and non-official language 10

⇒ Francophones account for 2.5 percent of the territory's population.

⇒ Some 405 people speak French most often at home; another 540 speak the language regularly, including 270 anglophones.

⇒ According to the 2001 Census, over 3,000 Northwest Territories residents have some knowledge of both English and French.

> There are 670 section 23 rights holders in the territory, 75 percent of whom live in exogamous relationships.[59]

Although the number of francophones in the Northwest Territories is steadily increasing, their proportion of the overall population has dropped from 3.6 percent over the last 25 years. The highest concentration of francophones is found in the capital Yellowknife, which is home to almost 70 percent of all the Territory's francophones. Other communities can be found in Hay River, Fort Smith, Inuvik and Norman Wells. Nowhere do francophones constitute a major percentage of the population, the highest being 3.8 percent in Yellowknife. The separation of Nunavut from the Territories had no significant impact on the francophone population.

---

[58] *2001 Census.*
[59] *Les ayants droit au Canada*, p. 6.

Nova Scotia

A very brief history[60,61]

The earliest European colonists in the New World included a hundred French settlers who, in 1604, founded Acadia on the Bay of Fundy. A vibrant agricultural community took root and flourished, its numbers swelling to around 15,000 in just 150 years. Then, in 1755, the British decided to expel the Acadians—even though they had remained steadfastly neutral throughout the ongoing conflict between England and France. It was a brutal affair: three-quarters were eventually deported, their homes torched and their land confiscated. When they were finally allowed to return, restrictions were imposed to prevent their communities from ever thriving again. Despite the abominable conditions, though, Acadian culture survived; today, some 37,000 francophone Nova Scotians make up almost four percent of the province's population.

Education[62,63]

Prior to 1975, no official curriculum existed for French-language courses taught in Nova Scotia. That changed with the creation of a French section within the Department of Education. Six years later, in 1981, Bill 65 officially recognized the rights of Acadians and francophones to an education in French. The first school board that operated in French was formed the following year, but it wasn't until 1996 that the government created a province-wide French-language school board. Later, however, Acadian parents had to turn to the Supreme Court in order to force the provincial government to implement certain education-related measures. The parents won that case in 2003.

In 2007, the French-language school board provided instruction to over 4,000 students in 19 schools.

---

[60] *The Oxford Companion to Canadian History.*

[61] *Franco.ca*, 2005.

[62] Conseil scolaire acadien provincial, 2007.

[63] *Annuaire de l'éducation en français au Canada*, pp. 110–115.

Stats at a glance[64]

Total population 899,970
French mother tongue 36,740
English mother tongue 838,283
Other mother tongues 25,376

Residents who have French as a mother tongue
> *French only* *34,025*
> *French and English* *2,555*
> *French and non-official language* *125*
> *French, English and non-official language* *35*

⇒ Francophones account for 3.9 percent of the province's population.

⇒ Some 20,000 people speak French most often at home; another 13,000 speak the language regularly, including nearly 6,000 anglophones.

⇒ According to the 2001 Census, over 90,000 Nova Scotians have some knowledge of both official languages.

> There are nearly 12,000 section 23 rights holders in the province, 66 percent of whom live in exogamous relationships.[65]

French-speaking Nova Scotians account for over 15 percent of the population in four of 18 counties, and Acadians constitute the majority in several municipalities. They live mostly on Cape Breton Island and on the south coast; along with Halifax, these regions account for over 80 percent of the province's total francophone population.

Acadians and francophones live mainly in rural areas, although over 11,000 reside in the Halifax region and another 1,000 live in the regional municipality of Sydney, on Cape Breton Island.

---

[64] *2001 Census.*
[65] *Les ayants droit au Canada*, p. 6.

Nunavut

A very brief history[66,67]

Nunavut became Canada's newest territory on April 1, 1999. Its roots, however, are steeped in the history of Canada: like the Northwest Territories from which it was formed, its indigenous peoples first came into contact with Europeans who were pushing westward and northward in the 18th and 19th centuries in search of furs and other resources. Many francophones were among the newcomers, acting as guides, traders, clerks and interpreters, as well as running various trading posts. Commerce was controlled for generations by the Hudson's Bay Company, but cooperatives—which had played an important role among francophone settlers farther south—helped break the company's monopoly and open the door to political organization. Nunavut came into being as a result of a massive land claim by the Inuit, who make up more than 85 percent of its population.

Education[68,69]

The history of French-language education in Nunavut starts in 1982, when parents began lobbying the Northwest Territories government for a school. At the time, 23 francophone children were enrolled in the English-language Nakasuk school in Iqaluit. Ten years later, the government allowed French to be taught half the time in the school. When Nunavut was created in 1999, its new government agreed to build a francophone school; work was completed in 2001 and 38 students moved into École des Trois-Soleils, the most northerly French-language school in the world. In 2004, the francophone school board, *Commission scolaire francophone du Nunavut*, or CSFN, was created. As of 2007, the CSFN was proceeding with plans to introduce grades 10 to 12 into the school.

---

[66] *The Oxford Companion to Canadian History.*

[67] *Franco.ca*, 2007.

[68] Commission scolaire francophone du Nunavut, 2007.

[69] *Annuaire de l'éducation en français au Canada*, pp. 118–120.

Stats at a glance [70]

Total population 26,610
French mother tongue 435
English mother tongue 7,400
Other mother tongues 19,325

Residents who have French as a mother tongue

> *French only* *395*
> *French and English* *20*
> *French and non-official language* *10*
> *French, English and non-official language* *10*

⇒ Francophones account for at least two percent of Nunavut's population.

⇒ Over 200 people speak French most often at home, and another 180 speak the language regularly.

⇒ According to the 2001 Census, 1,010 residents of Nunavut have some knowledge of both French and English.

> There are 670 section 23 rights holders in the Northwest Territories/Nunavut, 75 percent of whom live in exogamous relationships. [71]

The 2001 Census was the first to study Nunavut's population separately from that of the Northwest Territories. The 2006 Census will provide a more comprehensive portrait of the francophone population in Nunavut.

According to statistics from the Nunavut Bureau of Statistics, there are 700 to 800 francophones in the territory, some 550 to 600 of whom live in Iqaluit—a proportion of one in 10 residents of the capital. Other statistics suggest that francophones in Iqaluit account for five percent of the city's population.

---

[70] *2001 Census.*

[71] *Les ayants droit au Canada*, p. 6.

Ontario

A very brief history[72,73]

French explorers reached southern Ontario in the early 1600s, although European settlement didn't occur in earnest until the following century. In the early 1800s, francophone communities sprang up between the Ottawa and St. Lawrence rivers, and in the southwest of the province. Francophones moved to Northern Ontario in the late 1800s and early 1900s. Wherever they went, French-speaking settlers built communities around the local church, much like their counterparts in Quebec. However, they soon forged a distinct Franco-Ontarian identity, which continues to evolve today with the arrival of francophone immigrants from other parts of Canada and the rest of the world.

Education[74,75]

The first French-language school in Ontario was opened in 1786 in present-day Windsor. The freedom to teach in French started to erode a century later, however, and reached its nadir in 1912 with the introduction of Regulation 17, which banned French from the classroom after Grade 1. In many respects, this restrictive measure helped forge the Franco-Ontarian identity as francophones from near and far joined forces to fight for their rights. Their efforts paid off: in 1927, the government stopped applying the regulation and in 1944 repealed it entirely. The government took several steps toward francophone governance of French-language schools in the second half of the 1980s. Then, in 1997, it created 12 French-language school boards, eight being Catholic and four public. In 2004, the Ministry of Education launched a vast initiative called *Aménagement linguistique* aimed at enhancing French-language education. In 2007, the 12 boards were administering some 400 schools throughout the province.

---

[72] *The Oxford Companion to Canadian History.*

[73] *Franco.ca*, 2007.

[74] Ontario Ministry of Education, 2007.

[75] *Annuaire de l'éducation en français au Canada*, pp. 122–166.

Stats at a glance[76]

Total population 10,642,790
French mother tongue 533,965
English mother tongue 8,119,830
Other mother tongues 2,672,080

Residents who have French as a mother tongue

> *French only* *485,630*
> *French and English* *37,135*
> *French and non-official language* *8,000*
> *French, English and non-official language* *3,200*

⇒ Francophones account for 4.7 percent of the province's population.

⇒ Some 326,000 people speak French most often at home, and another 203,000 speak the language regularly.

⇒ According to the 2001 Census, 1,320,000 Ontarians have some knowledge of both official languages; this figure represents 12 percent of the population, and has tripled in 50 years.

> There are almost 170,000 section 23 rights holders in the province, 57 percent of whom live in exogamous relationships.[77]

Over 200,000 Franco-Ontarians reside in the eastern part of the province, where they account for 20 percent of the population. That figure is considerably higher in some areas, and francophones form the majority in certain rural municipalities. Northern Ontario is home to over 120,000 francophones, or a quarter of the province's francophone population. In the southern part of the province, including the Greater Toronto Area, the Franco-Ontarian population has increased in pace with the economic development and through immigration. One francophone in five now lives here, although they represent only two percent of the general population.

---

[76] *2001 Census.*

[77] *Les ayants droit au Canada*, p. 6.

Prince Edward Island

A very brief history[78,79]

Prince Edward Island, like the entire Maritime region, was home to the Mi'kmaq well before the arrival of European explorers. Jacques Cartier reached the island in 1534; the French soon named it Île Saint-Jean, but didn't establish a permanent colony until 1720. The settlement remained small until some 30 years later, when its numbers swelled with Acadians from the mainland fleeing deportation by the British. However, many of the French-speaking islanders ended up leaving or being deported and, within a few years, PEI had become predominantly English.

Education[80,81]

The first Acadian school in PEI was opened in Rustico in 1815. Others soon followed, and their numbers steadily grew throughout the province. Things started to change for the worse in the 1950s, when the provincial government began a lengthy consolidation that culminated in the 1972 reorganization of 300 English and French school districts into five boards. Only one board was French; it could operate in just one part of the province, and within a few years it had just one school to govern. All the other Acadians on the Island simply lost the possibility to have their children educated in French. Only in 1990 did the board become responsible for French-language education across the province. In 1980, however, the government had approved a bill that created real obstacles for Acadians and francophones seeking a French education for their children. Less restrictive legislation was finally passed in 2000 following a Supreme Court ruling. As of 2007, the board was operating six schools in various parts of the Island.

---

[78] *The Oxford Companion to Canadian History.*

[79] *Franco.ca*, 2005.

[80] Commission scolaire de langue française de l'Île-du-Prince-Édouard, 2007.

[81] *Annuaire de l'éducation en français au Canada*, pp. 74–76.

Stats at a glance[82]

Total population.. 133,000
French mother tongue 6,105
English mother tongue 125,650
Other mother tongues 2,000

Residents who have French as a mother tongue
> › *French only* *5,665*
> › *French and English* *440*
> › *French and non-official language* *0*
> › *French, English and non-official language* *0*

⇒ Francophones account for 4.6 percent of the province's population.

⇒ Some 3,000 people speak French most often at home; another 2,000 speak the language regularly, including 1,000 anglophones.

⇒ According to the 2001 Census, 16,000 Prince Edward Islanders have some knowledge of both official languages.

> There are over 2,000 section 23 rights holders in the province, 66 percent of whom live in exogamous relationships.[83]

The francophone population of Prince Edward Island has been relatively stable since 1981. This stability despite a generally declining Island population is explained by the arrival of young French-speaking adults.

Today, seven out of 10 Acadians and francophones live in the western part of the Island in Prince County, where they account for 10 percent of the population. Most live in the Evangeline area and are the majority in a few villages. Other major francophone communities can be found in Summerside, St. Eleanors and Miscouche.

---

[82] *2001 Census.*

[83] *Les ayants droit au Canada*, p. 6.

Saskatchewan

A very brief history[84,85]

Francophones reached Saskatchewan in the late 17th century in the form of voyageurs taking part in fur-trading expeditions. Like their prairie counterparts farther east, these men often married local First Nations women, helping to create the Métis nation. The Catholic Church played a key role in these families' daily lives, helping them maintain their language and culture and providing French-language education. The most important influx of francophone immigrants, however, came in the late 19th and early 20th centuries with the introduction of farming to the region. French-speaking settlers came from Quebec and the Maritimes, sometimes after years spent in the United States, as well as from Europe. They mostly formed communities around French-language parishes; two of the larger settlements were Batoche and Gravelbourg.

Education[86,87]

Although French-language education was being provided when Saskatchewan came into being in 1905, it started to lose ground in 1909 and was banned entirely in 1931. Not until 1967 did the government once again allow the teaching of French in the province's classrooms. In 1988, francophones won a court ruling that recognized their right to French-language education and governance of their schools. Francophone Saskatchewanians, or Fransaskois, finally started to govern their education system in 1993, and by 1995 there were nine school boards throughout the province. This model was changed in 1998, and in 1999 the school boards were replaced by a single provincial francophone school division. In 2007, the *Division scolaire francophone* was offering a French-language education in 12 schools around the province.

---

84 *The Oxford Companion to Canadian History.*

85 *Franco.ca,* 2007.

86 Division scolaire francophone, 2007.

87 *Annuaire de l'éducation en français au Canada,* pp. 174–178.

Stats at a glance[88]

Total population... 963,150
French mother tongue.. 19,520
English mother tongue 827,355
Other mother tongues 126,045

Residents who have French as a mother tongue

> *French only* *17,775*
> *French and English* *1,375*
> *French and non-official language* *255*
> *French, English and non-official language* *115*

⇒ Francophones account for 1.9 percent of Saskatchewan's population.

⇒ Some 5,000 people speak French most often at home, and another 8,000 speak the language regularly.

⇒ According to the 2001 Census, over 49,000 Saskatchewanians have some knowledge of both official languages.

> There are 8,000 section 23 rights holders in the province, 75 percent of whom live in exogamous relationships.[89]

Most francophone families have been living in Saskatchewan for generations, a fact that has shaped their identity and sense of belonging. Nearly eight out of 10 Fransaskois were born in the province.

The number of Saskatchewanians whose mother tongue is French has declined significantly—by almost half—in the last 50 years. Almost two-thirds of Fransaskois are rural dwellers; in the cities, they number 3,500 in Saskatoon, 2,500 in Regina and 1,350 in Prince Albert. Many francophone institutions have been created in these areas, most often associated with a French-language school.

---

[88] *2001 Census.*

[89] *Les ayants droit au Canada*, p. 6.

Yukon

A very brief history[90][91]

The first Europeans to settle in the Yukon included francophones who came with the fur trade and Catholic missions. The *coureurs des bois* came north throughout the 19th century, adapting so well to life in the new land that French was often the language of choice for communication among francophones, anglophones and First Nations people. Francophones established a presence in the territory before the Klondike gold rush of the late 1890s, at which time there was a huge influx of prospectors from around the world, particularly the United States. The boom was short-lived, however, and not until the Alaska Highway was built in the 1940s did the population start to rebuild. Aboriginal Yukoners have fared very poorly over the years, particularly as a result of residential schools designed to assimilate the children into western society. Today, the First Nations make up only 20 percent of the Yukon's population, and a mere 10 percent of them speak their ancestral tongues.

Education[92][93]

In 1982, a group of francophone parents formed an association to lobby for French-language education in Whitehorse. They adopted a consultative approach with members of the English-speaking majority and, in 1984, a French program was started in the basement of an English school. Thirty-four students from grades 1 to 6 attended; in 1988, the program gained the status of a school, which in 1990 moved into its own temporary facilities. In 1995, the *Commission scolaire francophone du Yukon* was created, and a year later the school, called École Émilie-Tremblay, moved to its permanent location. As of 2007, it was attended by some 130 students from kindergarten to Grade 12.

---

[90] *The Oxford Companion to Canadian History.*

[91] *Franco.ca*, 2005.

[92] Commission scolaire francophone du Yukon, 2007.

[93] *Annuaire de l'éducation en français au Canada*, pp. 190–192.

Stats at a glance[94]

Total population.. 28,520
French mother tongue 1,060
English mother tongue 24,450
Other mother tongues 2,900

Residents who have French as a mother tongue

> *French only... 975*
> *French and English 85*
> *French and non-official language 0*
> *French, English and non-official language.............. 0*

⇒ Francophones account for 3.8 percent of the territory's population.

⇒ Some 430 people speak French at home.

⇒ According to the 2001 Census, 2,890 Yukoners had some knowledge of both French and English.

> There are 350 section 23 rights holders in the province, 71 percent of whom live in exogamous relationships.[95]

The number of Yukoners whose mother tongue is French more than tripled between 1951 and 2001. Not only have many francophones chosen to live in the Yukon, but a growing number choose to stay permanently.

Four francophone Yukoners out of five reside in and around Whitehorse, the territory's capital. Dawson City has the second largest francophone community, accounting for four percent of the total population.

About 10 percent of Yukoners have some knowledge of French, and 15 percent have francophone roots.

---

[94] *2001 Census.*

[95] *Les ayants droit au Canada*, p. 6.

Bibliography

Alberta Education. *School Councils Handbook: Meaningful Involvement for the School Community*. Edmonton, Rev. 1999.

_____. French Language Services Branch. *Affirming Francophone Education – Foundations and Directions: A Framework for French First Language Education in Alberta*. Edmonton, 2001.

_____. French Language Services Branch. *Programme d'éducation de maternelle — français langue première*. Edmonton, 1999.

Alberta Home and School Councils' Association. *Alberta School Council Resource Manual*. Edmonton, 2006.

Allard, Réal. "Le bilinguisme d'enfants de couples exogames et l'éducation en français: mythes et réalités," *ConnEXions*. Fédération des parents francophones de l'Alberta. Edmonton, 2005.

Allard, Réal, Carole Essiembre and Sylvie Arseneau. "The values and choices of exogamous couples," *ConnEXions*. Fédération des parents francophones de l'Alberta. Edmonton, 2005.

Association canadienne d'éducation de langue française. *Cadre d'orientation en construction identitaire*. Quebec City, 2006.

Association canadienne-française de l'Ontario. "L'avenir est à ceux qui luttent : Les Franco-Ontariens et le règlement XVII," *Francophonie ontarienne*. Toronto, 1999.

Canada. Department of Canadian Heritage. *Bilingualism: A Selling Point for Canada*. Ottawa, 1999.

_____. Department of Canadian Heritage. *Francophones in Canada: a Community of Interests*. New Canadian Perspectives. Ottawa, 2000.

_____. Department of Canadian Heritage. "French-language education in a minority setting: a continuum from early childhood to the postsecondary level," *Interim Report of the Standing Senate Committee on Official Languages*. Ottawa, 2005.

_____. Department of Canadian Heritage. *Guide to the Canadian Charter of Rights and Freedoms*. Ottawa, 1982.

_____. Department of Canadian Heritage. *Official Languages: Myths and Realities*. Ottawa, 1999.

_____. Department of Canadian Heritage. *Outlook by Province and Territory*. Ottawa, 2003.

_____. Department of Canadian Heritage. *The Canadian Experience in the Teaching of Official Languages*. Proceedings of the Symposium hosted by the Official Languages Support Programs Branch on May 22–23, 1996. New Canadian Perspectives. Ottawa, 1996.

_____. Human Resources Development Canada. *Family Literacy in Canada*. Ottawa, 2001.

_____. Office of the Commissioner of Official Languages. *School Governance: The Implementation of Section 23 of the Charter*. Ottawa, 1998.

_____. Office of the Commissioner of Official Languages. *Rapport Annuel, Édition Spéciale 35e anniversaire (1969-2004), Vol. 1*. Ottawa, 2004.

_____. Service Canada. *Facts on Canada*. Ottawa, 2007.

_____. Statistics Canada. *Nation Tables, 2001 Census*. Ottawa, 2002.

_____. Supreme Court of Canada. *Arsenault-Cameron v. Prince Edward Island*. Ottawa, 2000.

_____. Supreme Court of Canada. *Mahé v. Alberta*. Ottawa, 1990.

_____. Supreme Court of Canada. *Reference re Public Schools Act (Man.), s. 79(3), (4) and (7)*. Ottawa, 1993.

Canadian Parents for French (Alberta Branch), Fédération des parents francophones de l'Alberta, Alberta Learning (French Language Services Branch), and Association canadienne-française de l'Alberta. *What do I want for my child?*. Edmonton, 2000.

Cazabon, Benoît. "L'aménagement linguistique : le cas de la francisation," *Éducation et francophonie*, Vol. XX:2. Association canadienne d'éducation de langue française. Quebec City, 1992.

Champagne, Madeleine. *Langue et culture : clés premières de la réussite scolaire à l'école de langue française en milieu minoritaire.* Fédération canadienne des enseignantes et des enseignantes. Ottawa, 2005.

Churchill, Stacy. *Official Languages in Canada: Changing the Language Landscape.* New Canadian Perspectives. Department of Canadian Heritage. Ottawa, 1998.

Collège universitaire Glendon and TFO. *Francophonies canadiennes : Identités culturelles.* Toronto, 2000.

Commission nationale des parents francophones. *Bonjour ! Helping bilingual families feel at home in French.* Saint-Boniface, 2002.

_____. *Seven ingredients to make a "French recipe" at home.* Saint-Boniface, 2001.

Council of Ministers of Education. *Programme for International Student Assessment.* Toronto, 2007.

Cummins, Jim. *Immersion Education for the Millennium: What We Have Learned from 30 Years of Research on Second Language Immersion.* Ontario Institute for Studies in Education of the University of Toronto. Toronto, 2000.

Cyander, M. and Frost, B. "Mechanisms of brain development: Neuronal sculpting by the physical and social environment," *Developmental Health and the Wealth of Nations.* New York: Guilford Press, 1999.

Dalley, Phyllis. "Héritiers des mariages mixtes : possibilités identitaires," *Éducation et francophonie*, Vol. XXXIV:1. Association canadienne d'éducation de langue française. Quebec City, 2006.

Daveluy, Michelle. "L'exogamie langagière en Amazonie et au Canada," *Anthropologie et Sociétés.* Quebec City, 2007.

Fédération des communautés francophones et acadiennes du Canada. *Découvrez la Francophonie canadienne.* Ottawa, 2007.

Fédération des parents francophones de Colombie-Britannique. *Historique de 1793 à aujourd'hui.* Vancouver, 2007.

Fédération des parents francophones de l'Alberta. *L'élève francophone au cœur de la communauté.* Edmonton, 2001.

Fédération nationale des conseils scolaires francophones. *Annuaire de l'éducation en français au Canada.* Ottawa, 2006.

_____. *Les ayants droit au Canada selon les groupes d'âge, la composition linguistique des couples, le revenu familial et le niveau d'éducation des parents.* Ottawa, 2004.

Gaudreau, Pierrette. "My child goes to French school: What role should I play?," *ConnEXions.* Fédération des parents francophones de l'Alberta. Edmonton, 2005.

Humanities and Social Sciences Federation of Canada. "HSSFC Working Group Hopes to Craft National Language Strategy," *Perspectives, Special Congress Issue.* Article issued as part of Congress 2001 — The modern languages. Quebec City, 2001.

King, Kendall and Fogle, Lyn. "Bilingual Parenting as Good Parenting: Parents' Perspectives on Family Language Policy for Additive Bilingualism," *The International Journal of Bilingual Education and Bilingualism,* Vol. 9, No. 6. Washington DC, 2000.

Lambert, Wallace E. "Issues in Foreign Language and Second Language Education," *Proceedings of the First Research Symposium on Limited English Proficient Student Issues.* Office of Bilingual Education & Minority Languages Affairs. Washington DC, 1990.

Lambert, Wallace E. and G. Richard Tucker. *Bilingual Education of Children: The St. Lambert Experiment.* Rowley, MA: Newbury House, 1972.

Landry, Rodrigue. "Challenges facing Canada's francophone minority: a macroscopic perspective," *Canadian and French Perspectives on Diversity — Conference Proceedings.* Canadian Heritage. Ottawa, 2003.

_____. "La francité familioscolaire," *ConnEXions.* Fédération des parents francophones de l'Alberta. Edmonton, 2005.

_____. *Libérer le potentiel caché de l'exogamie. Profil démolinguistique des enfants des ayants droits francophones selon la structure familiale.* Institut canadien de recherche sur les minorités linguistiques/Commission national des parents francophones. Moncton, 2003.

_____. "Pour une pédagogie actualisante et communitarisante en milieu minoritaire francophone," *Actes du colloque pancanadien sur la recherche en éducation en milieu francophone minoritaire : Bilan et prospectives.* CRDE, Faculté des sciences de l'éducation of the Université de Moncton: Moncton, 2000.

Landry, Rodrigue and Réal Allard. "Beyond Socially Naïve Bilingual Education: The Effects of Schooling and Ethnolinguistic Vitality on Additive and Subtractive Bilingualism," *Annual Conference Journal,* National Association for Bilingual Education. Washington DC, 1993.

_____. "Diglossia, ethnolinguistic vitality, and language behavior," *International Journal of the Sociology of Language,* 108, (1994).

_____. "Ethnolinguistic Vitality and the Bilingual Development of Minority and Majority Group Students." In W. Fase, K. Jaspaert and S. Kroon (eds.), *Maintenance and Loss of Minority Languages.* Amsterdam: Benjamins, 1992.

_____. "L'exogamie et le maintien de deux langues et de deux cultures : le rôle de la francité familioscolaire," *La Revue des sciences de l'éducation,* XXIII, 3, (1997).

Landry, Rodrigue, Réal Allard, and Raymond Théberge. "School and Family French Ambiance and the Bilingual Development of Francophone Western Canadians," *The Canadian Modern Language Review/La Revue canadienne des langues vivantes,* (February 1991).

Mahé, Yvon. *L'École au cœur de la communauté, un partenariat essentiel.* Forum on partnerships in francophone education, Vancouver, 1997.

_____. "L'élève francophone au cœur de la communauté : Pour vivre des expériences et des apprentissages signifiants," *Le Chaînon,* Fédération des parents francophones de l'Alberta, 15, 3, (October 2001).

Martel, Angéline. "Langues, constructivismes et interculturalité. Comment participer à l'harmonisation des sociétés par l'apprentissage du français." *L'éducation en débats : analyse comparée*, Vol. 1, Télé-Université. Quebec City, 2003.

_____. *Rights, Schools and Communities in Minority Contexts: 1986–2002*. Ottawa, Minister of Public Works and Government Services Canada, 2001.

Masny, Diana. "Literacy Development in Young Children," *Interaction*, 21, (Spring 1995).

Mathieu, Daniel. "French in the Northwest Territories from Radisson to the Present Day." Paper presented at *On the Eve of the Year 2000, A Forum on French in the Northwest Territories*, La Fédération Franco-TéNOise. Yellowknife, 1999.

McCain, Margaret Norrie & J. Fraser Mustard. *Early Years Study: Reversing the Real Brain Drain*. Study prepared for the Ontario Children's Secretariat. Toronto, 1999.

Memorial University of Newfoundland. *French Presence in Newfoundland*. Saint John's, 1999.

Museum of New France — Canadian Museum of Civilization Corporation. *Our Ancestors of European Origin*. Hull, 2001.

National Committee for Canadian Francophonie Human Resources Development. *Francophone and Acadian Communities*. Hull, 2001.

O'Keefe, Michael. "Demographic Trends and the Minority-Language Communities in Canada," *Seventh Conference of Departmental Official Languages Champions*, Faculté Saint-Jean: Edmonton, 2003.

_____. *Francophone Minorities: Assimilation and Community Vitality*, 2nd edition. New Canadian Perspectives. Ottawa, Department of Canadian Heritage, 2001.

Ontario. Ministry of Education. *Aménagement linguistique — A Policy for Ontario's French-Language Schools and Francophone Community*. Toronto, 2004.

_____. Ministry of Education. *Politique d'aménagement linguistique de l'Ontario pour l'éducation en langue française, 2004.* Toronto, 2004.

_____. Office of Francophone Affairs. *Francophone Community of Ontario.* Toronto, 2007.

Organisation Internationale de la Francophonie. *The International Organisation of the Francophonie.* Paris, 2007.

Oxford University Press. *The Canadian Oxford Dictionary,* 2nd edition. Don Mills, 2004.

_____. *The Oxford Companion to Canadian History.* Don Mills, 2004.

Paiment, Lise. "Pourquoi inscrire son enfant dans une école de langue française?," *ConnEXions.* Fédération des parents francophones de l'Alberta. Edmonton, 2005.

Saskatchewan Education. *Francisation scolaire : Document d'orientation portant sur les mesures spéciales de francisation dans les écoles fransaskoises.* Regina, 2000.

The Canadian Encylopedia. Historica. Toronto, 2007.

Tougas, Janine. *Le français chez nous: Some practical ideas for the promotion of French in bilingual families.* Fédération provinciale des comités de parents du Manitoba. Winnipeg, 1999.

Trelease, Jim. *The Read-Aloud Handbook,* 5th edition. New York: Penguin, 2001.

Index